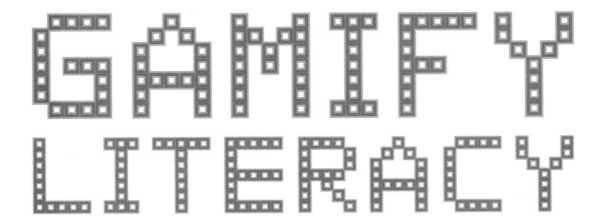

GAMIFY LITERACY

BOOST COMPREHENSION, COLLABORATION AND LEARNING

Edited by Michele Haiken

International Society for Technology in Education

PORTLAND, OREGON • ARLINGTON, VA

Gamify Literacy
Boost Comprehension, Collaboration and Learning
Edited by Michele Haiken

© 2017 International Society for Technology in Education
World rights reserved. No part of this book may be reproduced or transmitted in any form or by any means—electronic, mechanical, photocopying, recording, or by any information storage or retrieval system—without prior written permission from the publisher. Contact Permissions Editor: iste.org/about/permissions-and-reprints; permissions@iste.org; fax: 1.541.302.3780.

Acquisitions Editor: *Valerie Witte*
Editor: *Emily Reed*
Production Manager: *Christine Longmuir*
Copy Editor: *Corinne Gould*
Indexer: *Wendy Allex*
Proofreader: *Ann Skaugset*
Cover Design: *Edwin Ouellette*
Book Design: *Jeff Puda Book Design*
Book Production: *Jeff Puda Book Design*

Library of Congress Cataloging-in-Publication Data available

First Edition
ISBN: 978-1-56484-386-9 (paperback)
Ebook version available

Printed in the United States of America

ISTE® is a registered trademark of the International Society for Technology in Education.

About ISTE

The International Society for Technology in Education (ISTE) is the premier nonprofit organization serving educators and education leaders committed to empowering connected learners in a connected world. ISTE serves more than 100,000 education stakeholders throughout the world.

ISTE's innovative offerings include the ISTE Conference & Expo, one of the biggest, most comprehensive ed tech events in the world—as well as the widely adopted ISTE Standards for learning, teaching and leading in the digital age and a robust suite of professional learning resources, including webinars, online courses, consulting services for schools and districts, books, and peer-reviewed journals and publications. Visit iste.org to learn more.

Related ISTE Titles

Teaching Literacy in the Digital-Age: Inspiration for All Levels and Literacies, Edited by Mark Gura

Make, Learn, Succeed: Building a Culture of Creativity in Your School, by Mark Gura

To see all books available from ISTE, please visit iste.org/resources.

About the Editor

Michele Haiken, Ed.D. has been teaching literacy for twenty years. A lifelong learner, Haiken is a middle school English teacher and an adjunct professor of literacy at Manhattanville College in Purchase, NY. She is the author of the blog The Teaching Factor (**theteachingfactor.com**) where she shares ideas for digital technology and gamification in the classroom to build multiple literacies and bolster student success. A member of ISTE's Literacy PLN, she moderates **#ISTELitChat**, a monthly Twitter chat discussing digital literacy. Haiken has spoken on the subjects of literacy, technology, and gamification throughout the U.S.. She lives in Stamford, CT with her family. You can connect with her on Twitter **@teachingfactor**.

About the Contributors

Carrie Baughcum is an inspiration junkie, idea sharer, learning enthusiast, and most of all, a passionate believer that all children can learn, educators just need to find out how to facilitate their learning. She currently teaches sixth, seventh and eighth grade extended resource special education in Arlington Heights, IL where she uses creative thinking, classroom gamification, doodling, technology, and fun to enhance student learning and achievement. In addition to teaching, Baughcum presents at conferences on topics like gamification and sketchnoting. She writes on her blog at **carriebaughcum.com** and tweets **@heckawesome**.

Robert Matthew Daly was born and raised in Melrose, MA. A New Englander at heart, he enjoys American History, the outdoors, and his home town sports teams. Daly earned his bachelor's degree in communications from the University of Massachusetts Amherst. After relocating to New York, he attended New York University for his master's degree in social studies education. Daly teaches Middle School Humanities in Scarsdale, NY and lives in Westchester County, NY with his wife Lauren, and two children, Benjamin and Sadie.

Dr. Angela Elkordy is director, learning technologies and chair, learning sciences program at National Louis University in Chicago, IL. She has been a teacher educator and worked in PreK–12 contexts for almost two decades. Dr. Elkordy teaches, collaborates, and conducts research around teaching and learning in digitally-mediated spaces considering design-thinking, creativity, and makerspaces in education. She works to share the joy of innovative learning experiences, particularly for teachers, and their students in under-resourced and challenging contexts.

Scott R. Garrigan, Ed.D. has been an educator for 45 years, teaching K–12 for 20 years (elementary and secondary biology certification), leading technology in two school districts for a dozen years, and teaching as an adjunct, professor of practice, and assistant professor in the graduate educational programs of Lehigh University and Wilkes University. He programmed his first learning game in 1981, and he's taught graduate courses that relate game-based learning to intrinsic motivation. Garrigan earned his master's and doctorate in educational technology from Lehigh University. He is a frequent presenter at regional conferences like PETE&C and at national conferences like ISTE. He guided the ISTE endorsement of Lehigh's four-course, online Technology Use in Schools certificate program for its close alignment to ISTE Standards.

Kip Glazer, Ed.D. is a native of Seoul, South Korea who resides in California. She holds California teaching credentials in English, social studies, mathematics, health, and school administration. She is an experienced educator who won several teaching awards including the County Teacher of the Year and the 23rd Congressional District of California Inspirational Educator Award. For the past decade, she has provided professional development for other educators in the area of literacy and learning technologies. Glazer has also presented at numerous national and state conferences on technology integration. Recently, she consulted for The Kennedy Center ArtsEdge Program on creating a professional development program using tabletop role-playing games and game creation. She writes monthly blogs for the International Literacy Association. She is now a school administrator. She can be reached via email at mrsglazer@gmail.com or on Twitter **@kipglazer.**

Chris Hesselbein is an innovation strategist for the Lake Oswego School District near Portland, OR. His automated leaderboard system based on Google's suite of tools for education is helping teachers around the world gamify their classrooms. You can learn about that system and read more of his writing about gamification at **www.insertcoin.org** Most often you can locate him on a mountain in the Pacific Northwest. All other times you can find him on him on Twitter **@ChrisHesselbein.**

Ivan Kaltman joined Teach for America in 1991 and taught fourth grade for two years in rural Louisiana. He continued working in education as a school-based occupational therapist in New Jersey. He is the coach of his school's Positive Behavioral Support in Schools program (PBSIS), which has been recognized by NJ PBSIS as a Showcase School. He recently became a videogame developer, with his first title, *Sydney's World,* making its commercial debut in 2016.

Sheena Kelly is a secondary librarian at Peak to Peak Charter School. With an undergraduate degree from Rice University in philosophy and a masters degree in library and information science from the University of Denver, Sheena has a never-ending thirst for inquiry and continuing education. She has presented at local, statewide, and national professional development conferences on library advocacy, mobile applications, and digital storytelling. Kelly has won numerous grants to bring technology and enhanced collections into her library, but it's her love of gaming that really fuels her brainship.

Mallory Kessen is a middle school English teacher in Ohio working toward her masters in computers and technology in education. She is the founder of Gamindex (**gamindex.org**), an online resource that connects teachers to video games for education. A gamer since she played *Pokemon Red* in grade school, Kessen loves any game with a great story and well-written characters. Contact her on Twitter **@mallorykessen** or email her at mallorykessen@gamindex.org.

MJ Linane is a high school teacher at Old Rochester Regional High School in Mattapoisett, MA. He was awarded the Massachusetts 2015 Pathfinder Award for advancing education technology in his district while still teaching in the classroom. He has been featured by companies Schoology and Peardeck. Linane is also a member of the Communication Committee of MassCUE, the state affiliate of ISTE. He can be found discussing education technology at his website, **guildway.com**.

Kristie Orlando-Bangali is a middle school Spanish teacher in Westchester, NY. She has been teaching for 11 years and is the coauthor of the Spanish curricula at Rye Middle School. She lives in Hawthorne, NY with her family.

Travis Phelps is a vice principal at St. Justin School and an adjunct at SCU's Academy of Blended Learning. He has been an EdCamp Lead Organizer, a Google certified trainer, a CUE Rockstar Faculty, a BloomBoard Contributor, and Edmodo Spotlight Fellow. He has been mentioned in *Flipped Learning for English Instruction,* featured in the Educators Lead podcast, and included in LinkedIn's "100 California Educators to Follow." He can be found on Twitter **@TravisPhelps80** or seen with his beautiful wife and three energetic children.

Rachelle Dene Poth is a Spanish and STEAM teacher at Riverview Junior Senior High School in Oakmont, PA. Also an attorney, Poth earned her Juris Doctor degree and recently a master's degree in instructional technology from Duquesne University. She enjoys presenting at conferences on technology and innovative ways to benefit student learning. Poth serves as the communications chair for the ISTE Mobile Learning Network, a member at large for Games & Sims, the innovations and resources co-chair for the Teacher Education Network, and the PAECT historian. Poth is proud to be involved in several communities including being a Common Sense Media educator, Amazon Inspire educator, WeVideo Ambassador, Edmodo Certified Trainer, Nearpod Certified Educator and PioNear, and ambassador for several networks. She enjoys blogging and tweeting **@rdene915**.

Tisha Richmond is a high school culinary arts teacher and Discovery School lead teacher at South Medford High School in Southern Oregon. She is passionate about creating an immersive classroom environment and finding innovative ways to make learning come alive for all students. Richmond has also developed and implemented a plan to gamify the high school staff. She is a member of the Oregon Department of Education Edtech Cadre, Southern Oregon Edtech Cadre, MSD549c Edtech Cadre, and South Medford High School Edtech Cadre. She moderates **#XPLAP** chat for Michael Matera, author of *Explore Like a Pirate*. She has presented gamification sessions and workshops regionally and out of state. Redmond teaches in a 1:1 iPad classroom and loves integrating technology into the classroom, creating an environment where students are continually demonstrating their learning in innovative ways. Find out more at **theconnectedculinaryclassroom.weebly.com** and on Twitter **@tishrich**.

Aaron Vanek has participated in live action role playing for nearly 30 years. He is the editor of *LARP World Magazine* (**larpworldmag.com**), co-creator of the Larp Census. He has designed interactive experiences for the Girl Scouts of America, the West Hollywood Book Fair, Sanrio, Inc., the UCLA Game Lab and the San Diego Public Library, among others. He created 17 edu-LARPS for schools and consulted for Texas State University on their nursing simulation program. Vanek currently teaches analog game design to junior high school students in Beverly Hills and serves as the vice-president of the 501c3 non-profit, The Game Academy (**thegameacademy.org**).

Shawn Young is the co-founder and CEO of Classcraft (**classcraft.com**). A former high school teacher, Young created *Classcraft* to have more fun with his students and help them succeed in school. He is the lead game designer, lead developer, and education specialist at Classcraft Games. Young's main focus is ensuring *Classcraft* reaches its fullest potential by using play, engagement, and collaboration to create a truly positive force in the classroom.

Contents

SECTION 3

Cheats: Gamification Strategies for Success

GAMIFICATION GLOSSARY

avatar. An icon, character, or figure representing a player in the game.

badge. A distinct token or symbol used to reward participation or achievement. Badges are earned by completing tasks or meeting specific criteria.

Bartle's Game Personas. Categories created by Richard Bartle in 1996 to classify gamers based on their gaming style and behaviors. Categories include: Achievers, Explorers, Gladiators and Socializers.

> **achievers.** Players who prefer to gain points, levels, and badges to show off their skills and status.

> **explorers.** Players who prefer discovering areas, creating maps, solving puzzles, or learning about hidden places and unknown glitches.

> **gladiators.** Players who thrive on competition, the thrill of competition, or hunting weaker players.

> **socializers.** These players participate for the social aspect of playing with, and against, others.

boss battle. A "boss" in gaming is a villain the hero must face and defeat to advance or win. The player utilizes his or her skills and abilities to defeat the boss.

coins. Points or rewards, either literal or fictional, used to represent levels or ranks in the game.

Easter egg. An intentional message, treasure, or quest hidden within the game for players to find.

gamification. The use of game mechanics in non-game settings to increase efficiency and engagement.

guild. A group of people who band together to achieve a common goal.

HP or health points. A player's life energy or what they need to remain active in the game.

LARP. Stands for live action role-play. Participants physically act out their character's actions.

leaderboard. The ranking of players according to points or completion of tasks.

level up. The act of a character or player advancing to the next level of ability or status within the game.

mission. A task that a player or team of players must complete in order to gain a reward.

quest. A series of tasks that a player or team must complete in order to gain a reward.

RPG. Stands for role-playing game, a type of game in which players assume the roles of characters in a fictional setting.

side quest. A quest that is not part of the main quest or game, but offers a side story or reward for completion.

XP or experience points. Points earned by participating in various experiences, challenges, and quests.

Foreword

The Sky's the Limit...

The imaginations of today's students are as endless and filled with possibilities as ever. As teachers, we need to tap into their imaginations more often. Students of all ages want to be a part of something larger than themselves, part of a team that is striving for a goal and finding challenges and mystery along the way. As gamers, they already tackle challenges, from complex decisions to implementing a strategy for the long-term win. While today's students may seem apathetic toward school, their attitudes toward the challenges in games are decidedly positive. As gamers, they are high-functioning, multitasking marvels ready to face any difficulty. They are willing to take risks and are resilient in the face of unrelenting challenges and the inevitable failures that accompany them. In my experience, when the gamer shows up to class, they're more than ready to succeed in the challenges of academia and the world beyond.

As such, it is important for us to take a closer look at the design elements of games and think about intentional and meaningful ways we can apply them to our teaching. Thinking like game designers and applying game mechanics to our classroom can radically shift how our students perform, act, and achieve. Ultimately, the game can help our students learn much more than just content. A well designed course, just as a game, can help reveal hidden talents, new preferences, and, best of all, an ever-growing sense of self. Humans have been playing games since our first steps on earth. It is the most natural way to learn just about anything and it is about time we embrace the natural and effective strategy of game design principles within our schools and classrooms. Game and the playful spirit that they elicit allow our minds to be free to explore, connect, and create in ways that have no end. As teachers, and hopefully game designers, we can create a better connection both with and for our students.

Gamify Literacy is a collection of ideas and testimonies from teachers who use gamification and game-inspired course design to further their mission as educators. As you begin to learn these techniques you will see the true power of building a fully immersive learning environment for your students. You will seek resources to help you design and create a motivating and challenging game experience. When you do need those resources, *Gamify Literacy* will no doubt be one you will be glad to have in your arsenal.

It is my hope that this is only the first step in your journey to build a dynamic course that infuses the most motivational, as well as inspirational, techniques of games into your classroom design. Once you start, I promise, you and your students will be forever changed!

Michael Matera

Author of *Explore Like a Pirate: Gamification and Game Inspired Course Design to Engage, Enrich, and Elevate Your Learners*

Introduction

By MICHELE HAIKEN

Today, all teachers are considered literacy teachers. Literacy, in all of its dimensions, is the ability to construct meaning from reading, writing, speaking, and listening. Literacy is a lifelong development and we continuously build on our understanding of these complex skills each day. Throughout school, students are interacting with texts (print, visual, digital) to make meaning, build knowledge, and develop an understanding of the world and all its intricacies. For some, this process can appear to be no more than consuming information only to be tested and assessed in order to graduate to the next grade level. Information disseminates from textbooks, PowerPoint presentations, and is regurgitated into worksheets and five-paragraph essays. Sounds boring, right? Maybe you're picturing the scene in *Ferris Bueller's Day Off* when the economics teacher is trying to solicit responses from the students and most are not even engaged. Ben Stein's character states in a monotone voice:

> In 1930, the Republican-controlled House of Representatives, in an effort to alleviate the effects of the... Anyone? Anyone?... the Great Depression, passed the... Anyone? Anyone? The tariff bill? The Hawley-Smoot Tariff Act? Which, anyone? Raised or lowered?... raised tariffs, in an effort to collect more revenue for the federal government. Did it work? Anyone? Anyone know the effects? It did not work, and the United States sank deeper into the Great Depression. Today we have a similar debate over this. Anyone know what this is? Class? Anyone? Anyone? (Hughes, 1986)

Introduction

Thus, the challenge is for teachers to make learning informative, engaging, student driven, and collaborative so students are interacting with information, and asking driving questions they solve themselves. Project-based learning and technology have allowed students and teachers to build literacy-rich learning experiences that encompass critical thinking skills and creativity, and "prepare students to be successful in the various dimensions of their lives" (Gura, 2014). And gamification and game-based learning aligns with these same strategies. Gamification is about transforming the classroom environment and regular activities into a game. It empowers creativity, collaboration, and play.

There are numerous ways to bring games and game playing into any content area classroom to promote learning and deepen student understanding. Whether teachers are looking to integrate an aspect of gaming into their class or utilize a game platform across the curriculum, they can introduce elements of gamification to enhance learning and student engagement, tap into Common Core State Standards (CCSS), and address the ISTE Standards for Students. Effective gamification promotes problem solving and collaboration. Games allow a safe place for failure, since failure is an essential source of feedback and learning. Few players quit a game after they lose—their first instinct is to play again to figure how to win the game. We want our students to show grit and continue playing even when learning gets challenging or failure happens.

Gamification isn't about completing worksheets for points, or as Vicki Davis, author of CoolCatTeacher Blog describes, "chocolate covered broccoli." Facts and information are used as tools for learning and assessment in gamification. Effective games are customized to different learners and students are encouraged to take risks and seek alternative solutions to show what they know. In today's classrooms, it's not only about learning content material—students must experience and build the necessary skills to become creators, innovators, and problem solvers in order to develop critical thinking and improve academic achievement. Applying gamification to reading, writing, speaking, and listening enriches the learning experience for students and promotes thinking "outside of the box" for both teacher and students.

Game theorist, author, and professor, James Paul Gee writes about the elements of good video games and how educators can incorporate these elements in schooling and learning. He states, "challenge and learning are a large part of what makes good video games motivating and entertaining. Humans actually enjoy learning, though sometimes in school you wouldn't know that" (Gee, 2007). In nagivating high stakes testing, many teachers have put fun aside for skill-and-drill test preparation.

2

Game-based learning and gamification support critical thinking and diverse learning styles through techniques like cooperative learning, players as producers, problem-based learning, and risk-taking.

Gamify Literacy has emerged from my own interest in gamification and my role as a literacy teacher. Three years ago, I attended a local edcamp and went to a workshop on gaming. The person leading the class was an English teacher like myself, and he shared how he used gamification to teach vocabulary. He shared a game platform called *Classcraft* where each of his students is assigned an avatar and every week students are assigned to write a diary entry from the perspective of the avatar about his or her adventures. The key is that the students have to use weekly vocabulary words in their diary entries from *Wordly Wise Workbooks,* a traditional vocabulary workbook. The more vocabulary words students incorporate into their stories, the more game points they earn. At that moment, I was hooked on gamifying learning. I was enamoured with *Classcraft's* game platform and the ability for this teacher to develop a creative writing assignment that incorporated rote vocabulary instruction in an exciting way. That edcamp session was a catalyst, like finding an Easter egg that unlocked the unlimited possibilities to teaching, collaboration, and experienced-based learning. I left armed with more questions than answers to how I might bring similar elements of gamification into my own classroom.

I had already been using Think Tac Toes and dabbled in QR code quests, played games on Kahoot, and human Scrabble. Yet, the idea of gamifying my entire class was my quest. I piloted *Classcraft* that spring with my class. I enlisted the gamers in my classroom to help me set up the game and give the other students some pointers for playing, and we got started. I read gaming theorists like Paul Gee and watched TED Talks by Gabe Zichermann (2011) and Brenda Romero (2011) on gaming. Michael Matera's *Explore Like a Pirate* (2015) offered hands-on, adaptable ideas for my classroom that helped me boost gaming experiences with my daily lessons. Weekly Twitter chats for **#XPLAP** (Explore Like a Pirate) and **#games4ed** extended my thinking and connected me with remarkable teachers around the globe who were also integrating games and gamification into their classrooms to boost content understanding and promote fun and learning. The weekly chats allowed me to interact with other gamemasters who experimented, integrated, and inspired my own gamification journey with my students. It was during one of our weekly Twitter chats when I tweeted, "We should collaborate on a book to share with the world all the amazing things this group is doing." And that tweet is now a reality. One of my objectives in curating this book is to help educators navigate through game-based learning and gamification, and adapt and adopt gaming strategies that engage students in literacy learning.

This book is organized in three sections. The first section, "Sandbox," includes gamification strategies that can be adapted to any content area classroom. Sandbox is a gaming term that is used to describe an open-ended, go-anywhere style of play employed in games. The chapters in this section address gamification as a classroom tool to promote learning. Sheena Kelly describes how she has gamified research projects with her fifth and sixth grade students. Students must carry out a mission to save the Veritas Galaxy from the Luddites with their brainship. In Aaron Vanek's chapter we learn about live action role-play (LARPing) in the classroom to boost student learning, build communication skills, and teach problem solving. Kip Glazer shares how she creates traditional board games with her ELL students for review and practice of key content area concepts and knowledge. Two of her students' game ideas (LitTwister! and Literary Clue: A Game of Whodunit?) inspire new ways to rethink classroom review and skill practice. In Tisha Richmond's chapter, we learn about the MasterChef missions, badges, and mini challenges she designs for her culinary arts students. Through gamification she is able to inspire creativity, independent learning, and collaboration while students build culinary skills and knowledge. Carrie Baughcum offer's key advice for getting started with gamification. She describes for readers her own process of gamifying the classroom and considerations for successful integration of games and gamification.

Section Two, "Homebrews and Game Sharks" includes descriptions of gaming activities from a wide variety of content area teachers that can be easily adapted for any classroom. Each chapter includes a description, information why to use it, the ISTE Standards that match the learning tool, instructions for how to use it, and examples from classroom teachers. Rachelle Dene Poth shares a scavenger hunt she created for her Spanish students. Robert Daly describes a World War I simulation using *Minecraft,* and Travis Phelps explains how and why to use the game platform, *Classcraft.* An interview with Shawn Young, co-founder and CEO of Classcraft follows Travis' chapter. I have also shared examples of an *Amazing Race* challenge I created based on Harper Lee's *To Kill a Mockingbird* that requires students to work cooperatively to gather clues, complete tasks, and articulate their understanding of the text. I also include chapters on boss battles and adventure quests. Quests can be any mini project students work on independently, and in this chapter I share a trivia adventure quest-based on current events. Kristie Orlando-Bangali shares how she uses the game *Grudgeball* in her classroom as a review and cooperative learning activity. Ivan Kaltman describes *Sydney's World,* a RPG computer game he created about a young girl looking for her father. Players read the story line of the game in order to successfully use strategies to win the game. Games take on many forms from board games, games to be played on SmartBoards, to digital gaming tools and apps. Games are always evolving, expanding, and emerging as per teacher vision and learning outcomes.

The last section of the book, "Cheats," taps into gamification strategies. Cheats are special codes that allow players to bypass the normal limitations of a game. Typical cheats allow you to gain extra lives, become invincible, and access different stages. Some cheats are built into games, while others only can be accessed using devices like the GameShark. This section includes details about designing effective leaderboards from Chris Hesselbein. Chris addresses the benefits and weaknesses of using leaderboards as a motivational tool for student gamers. Both Angela Elkordy and MJ Linane write about digital badges as gamification tools. Borrowing from the Girls Scouts, Boy Scouts, and the military, badges can be a tool for motivation and even used to map out learning outcomes for students to attain mastery. Scott Garrigan addresses gamification as a way to enhance student motivation and learning through a deeper understanding of game and gamification concepts.

How you read this book is up to you. You can read it from cover to cover, adapting the games and gamification tools described in each chapter. Or you can peruse the chapters in isolation using the tools and content for your own classroom. Literacy strategies are embedded throughout. When I first set out to create this book, it was to bring together some of the educators, researchers, practitioners, and game designers who inspired me to gamify my own classroom. The contributors of the book teach a wide variety of students from an array of content areas, and many are not just content area specialists, but literacy advocates who use gamification to coach students to be successful readers, writers, and critical thinkers. Teachers must continue to equip students with literacy skills needed to participate, engage, and succeed in our global and digital society. We learn by doing and by making things our own. Gamification is an approach to learning that connects meaningful gaming with content objectives. All of the material presented in the book is adaptable for diverse student learners and across content areas. Model, adapt, play, reflect, revise, and play on. This book was designed to inspire, power up, and boost the love of learning.

Reading far and wide on gamification, participating in weekly Twitter chats, attending ISTE and other game-based conferences, I was inspired to gamify my classroom. With the help of my professional learning network (PLN), and my own students who are video game fanatics, my evolution as a teacher and gamer leveled up from

Jeopardy PowerPoint games to full-on immersion in *Classcraft,* designing adventure quests, scavenger hunts, and boss battles with each inquiry unit I taught. And yet, there is so much more to learn and do. As I write this introduction and reread each chapter, I'm mapping out a dystopian quest with badges for my students to complete during a dystopian reading unit. My hope is that the ideas presented in this book will activate your own thinking about content area learning and literacy in your classroom, and that gamification is a strategy that inspires students to take charge of their own learning.

Ready.

Set.

Game on.

References

Davis, V. (2014). Gamifying Education: Do We Know How to Gamify the Classroom? *The CoolCat Teacher Blog.* Retrieved from http://www.coolcatteacher.com/gamifying-education/

Gee, P. (2007). *What Video Games Have to Teach Us About Learning and Literacy* (2nd ed.). New York, NY: Palgrave Macmillian.

Gura, M. (2014). *Teaching Literacy in the Digital Age: Inspiration for all levels and literacies.* Eugene, OR: ISTE.

Matera, M. (2015). *Explore Like a Pirate: Gamification and Game Inspired Course Design to Engage, Enrich, and Elevate Your Learners.* San Diego, CA: Dave Burgess Consulting, Inc.

SECTION 1

Sandbox
Open-Ended, Go-Anywhere Style of Play

1

School Research Goes Galactic

> Using Game Design to Reimagine Middle School Research Projects

By SHEENA KELLY

A colleague recently asked me, "What *is* gamification?" The first metaphor that sprang to mind was today's retail shopping experience. Starbucks gamifies your coffee drinking experience by giving you points and rewards for buying drinks, food, and other merchandise. Local grocery stores gamify the chore of grocery shopping by offering special pricing on your favorite foods and giving pennies off your next gas purchase. I'm sure you can think of even more examples of gamification and other incentive systems at play in the everyday activities of your life. The widespread use of games and gaming in our society, means that my middle school students have grown up earning points and rewards for completing everyday tasks.

Prepare to Blast Off!

I grew up as the first console gaming systems were just hitting the retail market. I remember plugging a joystick into my grandfather's Commodore 64 computer, and I still play my original Super Nintendo gaming system. During my secondary school years, the concept of making mundane tasks into fun and engaging games was not a part of people's everyday experiences. But as far back as I can remember, I have owned at least one gaming console. Today, I own seven different devices to play games on. And today's students are even more likely to own gaming consoles earlier in their lives. In the book *Hanging Out, Messing Around, and Geeking Out: Kids Learning with New Media*, the authors state, "Gaming represents the central form of early computer experience for kids" (Ito et al., 2010). My gaming isn't confined to the computer, of course. I was raised playing all kinds of games with family and friends. I love board games like Sorry, card games like Fluxx, puzzle games like *Portal*, racing games like *Mario Kart*—really *all of the games*.

I knew I enjoyed games, and I knew my students enjoyed games. I wanted to gamify my research curriculum before I knew what that meant. What I was only vaguely aware of is the fact that "games and simulations yielded better attitudes toward learning when compared to traditional teaching methods and seem to facilitate motivation across different learner groups and learning situations" (Kapp, 2012). And I needed all good attitudes and higher motivation to buy into the content I was peddling. Research projects are a necessary component in developing critical thinking, reasoning abilities, and information literacy skills. I could sense, however, that the middle school students were not fully engaged in the process of inquiry, and many were not fully grasping the concepts I was trying to teach. I knew something had to change. Through my research and experience I knew that "not only is game play time growing among U.S. youth, but forms of game play and gaming demographics are diversifying" (Ito et al., 2010). This trend has continued so much so that some game worlds have even been developed into movies. For example, the 2016 *Angry Birds* movie and the 2014 *Lego Movie* are two recent games turned into feature-length films. Even though my love of research was not a passion I could pass on to students, my love of gaming was.

The Veritas Galaxy

As the teacher librarian for grades 6-12, I have the opportunity to teach information literacy skills in collaboration with a variety of different departments. I work on Veritas most closely with middle school social studies teachers. I'm fortunate to work with a group of educators who, with few hesitations, jumped on board when I proposed, "What if we taught students how to research...but in space?" As a K-12 school, we can vertically align our information literacy skills instruction to ensure students graduate with a thorough understanding of how to find and retrieve information in a variety of formats, evaluate that information using several criteria (see Appendix A), and synthesize and apply that information in new contexts. With the classroom teacher's content knowledge and my understanding of the American Association of School Librarians Standards for the 21st-Century Learner, I built a world where truth was the highest value: The Veritas Galaxy (see Figure 1.1). At the heart of the game is the idea that a process of inquiry can lead to deeper understanding of the world around us. With every new Luddite encounter, students must ask good questions to propel them in their process of discovery.

The Story (so far)
In a galaxy pretty far from here...

...in a place that, until now, has never before been seen by human eyes...a malevolent entity is approaching.

The Luddites have been conquering planet after planet in the Veritas Galaxy, having destroyed the Milky Way centuries ago in the Fourth Galactic War. We are the last humans who can save the last galaxy which holds the ultimate truth.

The Luddites have been gathering their armies and they seek to harvest the resources on all of the planets in the Veritas Galaxy. Their insatiable quest for knowledge has led to the destruction of legions.

Only you, powering your Brainship, have the fortitude to face the Luddites as you explore the galaxy. Many challenges await you on your quest. Be strong. Be brave. Be curious.

Figure 1.1. Screenshot of backstory for Veritas Galaxy.

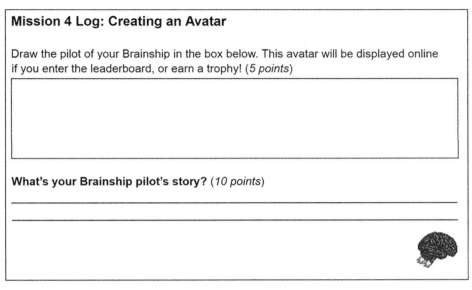

Mission 4 Log: Creating an Avatar

Draw the pilot of your Brainship in the box below. This avatar will be displayed online if you enter the leaderboard, or earn a trophy! (*5 points*)

What's your Brainship pilot's story? (*10 points*)

Figure 1.2. Creating an avatar student assignment.

The game progresses during students' research projects in social studies classes. As teachers introduce students to the assignment, I fly in to teach and enhance information literacy concepts and strategies. Despite my limited student contact, I effectively used backwards design to think through the research concepts that needed to be taught, the American Association of School Librarians (AASL) standards to cover, and overarching gameplay and story development.

In addition to teaching critical information literacy skills, I wanted to teach students about the importance of asking good questions and making informed decisions. I was, therefore, very intentional about the language and rhetoric I used in storytelling and gameplay. Some names are fictional (like Planet Meglaton, ruled by cat people) while some are intellectually meaningful. For example, corpus coins (which are dry pinto beans spray painted silver) can be earned by players during class time instruction for things like finding a typo on a mission data sheet or helping a fellow space traveller in need. Coins can also be lost when students are off task or don't follow instructions. In reality, the *corpus callosum* is the part of the brain that forms neural connections between the right and left hemispheres, which I didn't know before developing the Veritas Galaxy story arc. This thoughtful game-play mechanism helps to make the game universe more convincing and comprehensive. I know much more about celestial bodies and the human brain now than I ever thought I would because of the research done to develop a believable game plot. The game is currently being played in middle school class-rooms, though I envision a future expansion of the game (or some derivative form) for high school students.

The sixth grade is my first opportunity to begin information literacy skill instruction, and it's also where students first encounter the secondary library and the Veritas universe. Because of this, I teach a bonus lesson at the start of the school year about how to utilize the library's resources. During this lesson, students are asked to read and sign the Explorer's Creed (see Appendix B) and the rules of play. They then create their avatar and their character's backstory within the game (see Figure 1.2). Using avatars allows students to become personally invested in the game. I considered a few digital avatar creators: The Lego SigFig Creator (**sigfigcreator.thelegomovie.com**) and Marvel's Create Your Own Superhero (**marvel.com/games/play/31/create_your_own_superhero**) for example, but I found that students were more creative when they had to depend on their own brainships for ideas. This is an easy mission to get all students on the scoreboard and feeling successful. Though game points can be earned and lost individually, students may collaborate on missions during different project assignments.

After students develop their character and backstory, they take the Bartle Test to determine their gamer personality within the Bartle taxonomy of player types. After answering a series of questions about character behavior and in-game preferences, students are given their percentage identification of the following gaming styles: Achiever, Explorer, Gladiator, or Socializer. These results, which are accessible by the teacher, help to customize and differentiate the game depending on the student's results in each class. Bartle explains the four styles of gamers in the following way:

> **Achievers** "give themselves game-related goals, and vigorously set out to achieve them." Goals can be built into the game in the form of assessments (like boss levels) but don't have to be that big. Smaller components can be built in for players to unlock as they progress.

> **Explorers** "try to find out as much as they can about the virtual world." The game universe should be complex enough to not bore the Explorers. Don't feel, however, that you must have all of the details set in stone before beginning gameplay. Students can always discover or unlock new areas as the game progresses.

> **Gladiators** "use the tools provided by the game to cause distress to (or, in rare circumstances, to help) other players." A component of most games is the option of doing harm to another player. Think of the game *Sorry* where players are

encouraged to send their opponents back to the starting line. A little friendly rivalry will help keep Gladiators motivated and engaged.

> **Socializers** "use the game's communicative facilities...as a context in which to converse (and otherwise interact) with their fellow players" (Bartle, 1996). It's important to allow students time to talk and collaborate, and this is especially true for Socializers. Offer opportunities for students to interact with each other throughout the game. For example, the research projects I lead are done in pairs or small groups, but I try to facilitate additional mingling outside of these core partner groups.

These gamer categories can serve as a planning aid to individualize the game to suit differing player motivations in a whole-class setting.

After students have completed the Bartle Test (1996), they explore the online portal for the Veritas Galaxy (see Figure 1.3). The portal includes links to mission data: class presentations, handouts, and video, as well as the leaderboard and gamemaster profiles.

Developing the gameplay and the game universe happened for me, simultaneously—I was unable to separate the characters and missions from the mechanics of the game.

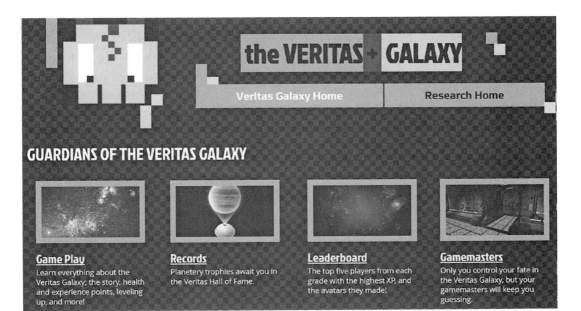

Figure 1.3. Screenshot of Veritas Galaxy portal.

As you start to develop your own game, you can think through strategic questions about your lessons, units, and activities within the world you're building.

Piloting Your Own Brainship

One of the most important parts of designing a game students want to play is creating a convincing world for it to take place in. You must take students far enough away from reality that the subject matter you're teaching blurs out of focus for them: the ultimate goal is to engage students in a way where they are more focused on the game (something fun) than being in class (something decidedly not fun), while still gaining the content knowledge and skills necessary for their academic success.

I suggest starting with the setting. Creating a vivid game universe makes it easy for students to get lost in the world, leading to deeper engagement with the content. I built my world in space for its limitless possibilities. We could travel with students to different moons and planets, get caught in an asteroid field, and we could encounter a myriad of fictional enemies and allies along the way. While it's not the most glamorous logo, the flying brain is the student's cue that they're about to embark on a new quest using their brainship. These details keep students interested in the experience while remaining slightly detached from reality.

When designing, think through different ideas and see which fits best with your content and educational goals. You could choose to build a world that is entirely fictional—played in an alternate dimension with creatures of your own design. Or your setting could be more realistic (space, for example) with a fictional storyline. Once you have identified a few potential concepts, think through the story arc of the game from start to finish (see Figure 1.4). Who is playing the game and how does play begin? Who or what is the player's enemy? How does the game progress and ultimately end? If you're struggling to identify rising action and pace of the game, it might be time to explore another idea.

The world you build should also consider the different learning styles of your students. While you can't appeal equally to everyone's sense of adventure, you can add elements within the gameplay that will appeal to a diverse group of students. Using the Bartle Test analysis of students' gamer personalities and knowledge of students' personal motivators, you can build in activities to support auditory, visual, kinesthetic, and tactile learners through different missions and quests. You're probably already using this style of differentiation in your regular classroom lessons, and you can be similarly intentional about building quests that appeal to these various learning styles.

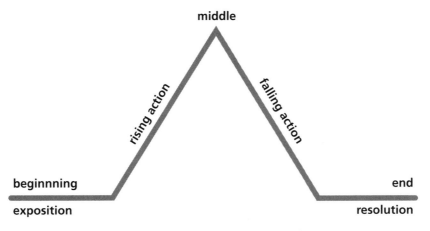

Figure 1.4. Story Map (NCTE, n.d.).

It's important for students to experience a measure of control over their destiny in the game. Their progress will include successes and "failures," which are all part of the process of inquiry. Each of these failures becomes the launchpad for discovery and understanding. The self-generated student buy-in that occurs when students create their brainship pilot's avatar and backstory is important as the gameplay progresses.

As important as failure is to the learning process, challenge and competition are equally important in appealing to a student's intrinsic motivators. In *The Art of Game Design,* Jesse Schell underscores the idea that "challenge is at the core of almost all gameplay" but challenges must be appropriately difficult for the learners (Schell, 2008). This is, again, differentiation you're likely doing in your regular classroom lessons. A more difficult concept to embrace is that the game should involve some competition amongst the players. As Schell notes, competition "allows for a balanced game on a level playing field...provides us with a worthy opponent...gives us an interesting problem to solve...fulfills a deep inner need to determine our skill level relative to someone else in our social circle...[and] allows for games involving complex strategy, choices, and psychology, all possible because of the intelligence and skill of our human opponent" (Schell, 2008). In Veritas, players compete for Bonus Brainship Battlepacks, a rank for the top five in each grade, and for the highest number of corpus coins earned.

At the end of the school year, when we celebrated the extra thrust power everyone's brainship got from so much learning, students had a huge sense of accomplishment over their progress. Each student has their avatar and earned level displayed during and end-of-year ceremony. Students are awarded a certificate and a space themed pencil. Though this is a small gesture, students appreciated being acknowledged in this way.

After a collaborative lesson with the sixth grade science teacher about website evaluation, some students responded very much in character. One student said, "I always love piloting my brainship through the galaxy and learning about the internet." Other students gave feedback of the experience that was more grounded in reality. As Ian said, "thank you for working with us! I learned to not trust the internet with everything" (which is the best review I could ever ask for). Students drew brainships and galaxies, and noted over and over again how much fun the lesson was (see Figure 1.5). My partner teachers have always reported higher engagement with their hard-to-focus students and a general sense of gratitude that they "didn't have to teach research."

Figure 1.5. Student example of personal brainship and galaxy.

Designing an Engaging Game Experience

Though the setting and characters for your game will determine many aspects of the game universe, there are a myriad of additional smaller details that are important to creating an engaging experience for student players. For example, the first lesson of the year has me, the "Skybrarian," dressed in gear from my tour in the fourth Galactic War. Though costumes are optional, think of fun things you can do to bring your game to life. Consider your game world using the following questions to guide your thinking:

1. **Where and when does the game take place? What different locations will players travel to, and how do they get there?**

2. **What characters do the students play? Are teachers part of the game or merely facilitators?**

3. **Who are the enemies and allies players will encounter during gameplay? How do these characters propel the story?**

4. **Is there a specialized vocabulary or language for your game universe? How do you communicate things like learning objectives and essential questions to students?**

5. **What elements of the story appeal to players different gaming and learning styles?**

6. **What does your game look like? Have you incorporated a custom font? What colors are found in your universe?**

Terms of Service

Before you begin plotting the mechanics of how your game is played, I recommend playing some games! Play different kinds of games to experience what you like and don't like about how games are played. What surprises or delights you about the game? What is frustrating to you during gameplay? A great source of inspiration for generating ideas is to look at what has already been done. As a corollary, don't let your imagination be limited by existing gaming conventions. Incorporate your school's mission and vision into your backstory. Utilize a classroom behavior policy when determining health points. Use reality to help you think through the fantasy world you are creating.

This is also an ideal time for collaboration between the full-time classroom teacher(s) and teacher librarians. The unique skills and perspectives brought to the table will help you to develop a consistent gaming experience for students that crosses the traditional boundaries that exist between content areas. As you'll see in the Explorer's Creed (see Appendix B), I made sure to build in language about rules changing at whim, just in case something needed to be tweaked (which has been and will continue to be important). This mechanism is also designed to encourage a mindset of lifelong learning and inquiry inherent in conducting good research.

The rules of your game should be simple to follow and understand. Students should feel abstracted from reality, not bogged down in a long set of rules that brings them right back to school. You also don't want students to run rampant in your newly minted universe. The Veritas Galaxy has only two explicit rules:

1. **Question everything with an open mind**

2. **Seek help when you get stuck**

There are other important things students must know and understand to play the game successfully, but the rules are short and simple, and they address many of the concepts I hope to teach during each mission.

Players progress through the game by leveling up during the course of gameplay. In the Veritas Galaxy, students earn truth points ("TP" for short, which middle schoolers appreciate) based on their performance on in-class work, formative assessment checks, completion of anticipatory-sets and closures, and performance on the final product of the research project. The accumulation of TP propels a student's brainship to a higher level in the game. Truth points are my version of experience points (XP) which is a common nomenclature in the gaming community. XP typically earned by players as they successfully complete missions and quests and determine a player's level in the game. As a game progresses and students level up, they may be able to unlock additional abilities or tools.

As mentioned above, students can also earn and lose Corpus Coins during classroom lessons. This is my version of health points (HP), which determine the health and life force of a player during the game. If there are adversaries in your game, encounters with the enemy will be a natural cause for HP loss but you can also use HP to reinforce desired classroom behavior.

Think through the game play using the following questions to guide you:

1. What medium is the game being played in? Do students complete worksheets and online assessments? Is there a physical game being played in class?

2. How do players learn more about the game? Is the game universe fixed or infinite? What are players able to contribute to the universe?

3. How does a player progress in the game? What are the different levels students can achieve? How many points does it take to get from one level to the next?

4. How many points should each unit, mission, or quest be worth? Will students be able to earn bonus points?

5. How do players earn and lose health points and experience points? How can you incorporate classroom management into these structures?

6. How can players check their progress and current point total?

Being a Gamemaster

My research curriculum is mapped to the American Association of School Librarians Standards for the 21st-Century Learner. These standards were instrumental in the design of my curriculum, especially given my limited instructional contact with students. As I planned each mission, I was cognizant of the particular skill I wanted to assess. This allowed me to design activities strategically and provide targeted feedback as part of the informal assessment process. As you design your game, map your standards to each activity. This is helpful information when sharing your lesson plans with other teachers at your school. If you decided to change or expand your game, having these standards explicitly mapped makes transferring this data to different missions easier. Once you have your game universe established, you can expand to additional grades, classes, or content areas.

Also important to the success of my curriculum is access to the digital tool NoodleTools (**www.noodletools.com**) through a district subscription. NoodleTools is a comprehensive research tool that reinforces the skills being taught in the game and gives students a structure to make their thinking visible. It allows students to collaborate on projects, and put the research and citation skills they've learned into practice. My favorite feature is the ability to share projects with the teacher. I'm able to check in on student progress throughout each research project and provide formative assessment in the form of comments to guide their research.

Game Over

Gamifying information literacy skills has helped me to be more successful reaching students who are not excited about conducting a research project. Through formative feedback, positive reinforcement, and a whole lot of fun, middle school students are experiencing the process of inquiry through wonder and space travel.

Appendix A

Source Evaluation with (ABC)²

Ask these ABC questions to verify information during research.

A: Authority
Who is the author of this information? What are their credentials or qualifications? If the source doesn't have an author, what can you find out about the organization that published it?

B: Bias
Why was this information written? Was it written to inform, persuade, entertain, or sell? Are arguments one-sided or do they represent multiple viewpoints? What other information has been published by this same author/institution?

C: Currency
When was this information published or last updated? Some information becomes dated when new research is available, but other older sources can be valid a hundred years later.

A: Appropriateness
What kind of tone, writing style, and vocabulary does this information reflect? Is the information readable for you and the intended audience? Does the author make any assumptions about the reader's prior knowledge?

B: Believability
How convincing is the information presented? Does it fit in with your other research? Does it have a bibliography or works cited so you can follow up for more on the information?

C: Context
Where does this information fit within the context of the rest of your research? Do you think there's enough evidence offered? Does your source appropriately cover the topic and add to your research?

Appendix B

The Explorer's Creed

By boarding and operating a spacecraft brainship, I _____
agree to honor the vastness of the space in my brain, and accept the maintenance
and tuning it will need on the journey. I vow to explore the reaches of the universe
with my brainship, openly and thoughtfully questioning everything I find along
the way. I am the captain of this vessel, and I will pilot this ship to the best of my
ability. Misuse of my brainship may result in undesired consequences, that I—as
captain of the ship—am prepared to accept.

I understand that the rules of the game can change at any time and without notice.
I will embrace these changes as the ever changing nature of the universe we play
in. I have read the Terms of Service and consulted the gamemasters with my
questions.

Game on!

Signature _____

Printed Name _____

Date _____

References

American Association of School Librarians. (2016). Standards for the 21st-Century Learner. Retrieved from http://www.ala.org/aasl/standards/learning

Bartle, R. A. (1996). Hearts, Clubs, Diamonds, Spades: Players who Suit MUDs. Retrieved from http://mud.co.uk/richard/hcds.htm

Ito, M., Baumer, S., Bittanti, M., Boyd, D., Cody, R., Herr-Stephenson, B., & Tripp, L. (2010). *Hanging Out, Messing Around, and Geeking Out: Kids Learning with New Media*. Cambridge, MA: MIT Press.

Kapp, K. M. (2012). *The Gamification of Learning and Instruction: Game-Based Methods and Strategies for Training and Education*. San Francisco, CA: John Wiley & Sons, Inc.

National Council of Teachers of English. (n.d.). [Plot Diagram]. Retrieved from http://www.readwritethink.org/classroom-resources/lesson-plans/plot-structure-literary-elements-904.html

Schell, J. (2008). *The Art of Game Design: A Book of Lenses*. Burlington, MA: Morgan Kaufmann Publishers.

2

LARPs for Learning

> Live Action Role-Play

By AARON VANEK

ISTE Standards for Students

1 Empowered Learner. Students leverage technology to take an active role in choosing, achieving and demonstrating competency in their learning goals, informed by the learning sciences.

3 Knowledge Constructor. Students critically curate a variety of resources using digital tools to construct knowledge, produce creative artifacts, and make meaningful learning experiences for themselves and others.

A timer ticks away precious seconds before the Praezorian warship recharges its primary guns and pummels us again. Our helm officer, normally a calm-faced Cetian, wrinkles her brow and pinches her lips in frustration—the ship's engines are too slow to maneuver us out of their range. A red light shrieking on my console indicates that it's damaged and inoperable. The shields are down. I draw a card out of the envelope for repair requirements: Engineering 3 skill and 1 Hyperonic Inductor. I bellow to the engineering section to bring an inductor to the bridge immediately or we're stardust. While waiting for salvation, I think, "What if I instead had to solve a math equation to fix this?"

Live action role-playing, or LARP (sometimes LRP in the United Kingdom), is an ancient, global art form with a terrible moniker, but we're stuck with it. Many people mistakenly think LARP descended from tabletop role-playing games like *Dungeons & Dragons,* which was first published in 1974 and is still popular in its fifth edition today. But there are examples of LARP-like activities such as mock trials, the Model United Nations, and military war games that predate *D&D*. In fact, the March 3, 1941 issue of *LIFE* magazine describes and photographs University of Nebraska students playing pretend in 19-year-old sophomore, Frederick Lee Pelton's imaginative planet Atzor, which he envisioned in 1934. Italy's Commedia dell'arte tradition of the 16th century could be considered LARPing, or a LARP precursor. I believe LARPs started when humans first donned animal skins and re-enacted the hunt.

LARP as an art form is different than traditional staged theater or role-playing games (RPGs), since, unlike theater, all participants are both actors and audience members, and everyone almost always has a degree of agency to alter the narrative outcome. For example, maybe Romeo and Juliet can live happily ever after in their LARP. LARPs are unlike tabletop RPGs since participants act out their deeds as opposed to narrating them to a gamemaster or as storyteller. In fact, some LARPs don't require a gamemaster at all. LARPs are not passive, but active—your experience hinges on the effort you and others put into it, as all participants work to create and sustain Johan Huizinga's "magic circle" (Huizinga, 1938).

Most LARPs around the world are created for entertainment purposes, like the introductory example, which I experienced in a Starship Valkyrie campaign. However, there's a growing international trend that uses LARPing to teach.

What is a LARP?

A LARP consists of two or more people each pretending to be someone or something else in a predetermined imaginary setting that takes place in a real location. These people interact with each other and the imaginary setting through improvisational acting for a set amount of time. In most, but not all, of these experiences, there is some degree of involvement from a gamemaster, who takes on a variable amount of control over the personalities of the pretend characters (who they are, what they want) and most of the imaginary setting (where it is, what it looks like, what's there). The gamemaster also may or may not be one of the characters. Through the interactions of everyone's imagination and improvisation, a narrative usually emerges. Participants don't do this for anyone other than themselves: there is no separate audience, everyone is a performer and a viewer (Vanek, 2009).

There are two fictions that participants need to make-believe to animate any LARP: an *external fiction* and an *internal fiction*. Believing an external fiction means you imagine that a classroom is an ancient Babylonian court, or a counter on a hexagonal grid indicates an alien spaceship circling for another attack. External fictions are what allow us to pretend we are not really where we seem, or the things we see, hear, and touch aren't what they are, but something else—something magical. It's much easier for most people to believe external fictions; we do it all the time when we watch plays or movies. Believing an internal fiction is harder. Internal fictions demand you believe that you're a starship captain, a valiant knight, a brilliant chemist, engineer, or President of the United States. Our characters might be ourselves but in a fictional setting. For example, you're you, but there are roaming zombies, or your character might be something entirely unlike you, like a plant creature that throws deadly spores when approached.

In a LARP, we wear a mask or a role to become a character that we briefly inhabit. These masks can be quite powerful for learning, since every mask bears at least some resemblance to the wearer, revealing what may be their best or worst qualities. Furthermore, walking, or role-playing, in another's shoes can be profound: the Crossroads Foundation (**crossroads.org.hk**) regularly runs simulations (LARPs under another name) for the World Economic Forum called *A Day in the Life of a Refugee*. According to one Ghanese refugee, "After watching TV, people may forget what they have seen. After doing this simulation, they will remember us" (WEF, 2014).

There are many different LARPs and types of LARPs that have occurred all around the world. Some are single events, like a movie—sometimes with reruns and sequels. Others are episodic, like a continuing story that occurs once a month, lasting years or even decades. The most popular genre of larp is fantasy, inspired by *Dungeons & Dragons*, but LARPS can also be post-apocalyptic, Western, horror, science fiction, historical, dramatic, comedic, satirical, musical, surreal, political, experimental, or combinations of these and more. Any topic suitable for a painting, novel, or song could be a topic for live action role-playing, as the breadth and depth of human experience is LARP-able.

Some LARPs persist merely five minutes in one sitting, others can last a month continuously, without breaking character. Most range from four to 48 hours. Live action role-playing is entering the mainstream with other fandom and gaming nerd cultural elements, so it should not be a surprise that this wonderful medium of expression is finally being acknowledged as an effective educational tool.

What Is Educational LARP, or Edu-LARP?

While live action role-playing has been used for centuries to instruct soldiers, the current use of LARP in curriculum is a recent development. While any experience can be educational, Malik Hyltoft draws a distinction between educational LARPs, or edu-LARPs, and regular LARPs suggesting, "In order for a larp to be educational, we would demand that the organizers of the activity have a plan for acquisition of knowledge or skills or correction of certain behaviours in the target group through the medium of the larp. So whilst the participants may feel like it is, the activity cannot be solely recreational" (Hyltoft, 2010).

Live action role-playing, or aspects of it, are already in the classroom under different names: experiential education, self-directed learning, situated learning, problem-driven or project-based learning, progressive inquiry, and gamified or process drama. Many teachers are already using simulations—which I consider to be a LARP—or costumed roleplay in the classroom outside of drama classes.

In his essay Hyltoft argues edu-LARPs are an effective teaching method because of distraction, motivation, activity, and power.

Distraction

According to Hyltoft, "Edu-larp works because it manages to distract the student from his daily life, thereby giving him a greater chance to concentrate on the subject at hand." In the same way that daily life can distract students from their schoolwork, participating in an edu-LARP can distract students from daily life (Hyltoft, 2010).

Motivation

Edu-LARP is effective because, "It places the students in situations where the motivation for doing school work is very clear and understandable" (Hyltoft, 2010). Hyltoft further breaks down this intrinsic motivation into three categories:

CHARACTER MOTIVATION
"It can be very hard to explain to a whole class of students with different interests and agendas, why some piece of abstract learning is relevant to them. It is much easier to create a character to whom it is relevant. As an example, most 15-year olds have no use for nuclear theory, but secret agents in the later part of World War II will memorize it gleefully" (Hyltoft, 2010).

NARRATIVE MOTIVATION

"A well made larp is like a good book, you cannot wait to see what is on the next page...when the subject matter becomes part of what they (students) need in order to act in the narrative setting, they are strongly motivated to learn it well and use it to the best of their ability" (Hyltoft, 2010).

META NARRATIVE MOTIVATION

This is when learning objectives can, be satisfied in the actual story or narrative, like math or algebra problems. In this case, "students are asked to participate in activities linked to learning objectives, and their performance in these activities is directly linked to some part of the edu-larp. For instance, on an edu-larp space journey, the navigation computer jams just as the spaceship is on collision course with an asteroid, and has to be reconfigured through the solving of vast amounts of relatively simple arithmetic so each student has to solve and hand in several pages of arithmetic" (Hyltoft, 2010). It should be obvious how this sentence in the essay was a eureka moment for me, who was already playing Starship Valkyrie.

Activity

The effectiveness of edu-LARP is in part due to its contrast to the traditional learning environment, where students are passively listening and reading. "Edu-larp works because it activates students in a school setting at an unusually high level (Hyltoft, 2010). Hyltoft further explains that the role and authority of the teacher in an edu-LARP is different than normal because "a teacher acting as a director cannot interfere with the actions of a student without breaking the narrative frame of the story solely because the actions of the students are not conforming to the ones expected or hoped for by the teacher—the interference has to be grounded in narrative modifications or game mechanics. The teacher/director has to conform to the frame of the narration and accept if the student tries out the boundaries of this frame, or even opts to fail within the context of the story" (Hyltoft, 2010). This allowance for failure is hugely important within the edu-LARP pedagogy.

Power

"Edu-larp works because it empowers the student, allowing him to make decisions and living with them. . . the student is given the freedom to act within the limits of the character" (Hyltoft, 2010). Allowing students to make decisions, and suffering the consequences of those decisions, is also a method of assessment, as teachers can gauge students' decisions and their work on being informed or uninformed.

Furthermore, a student might not acquire the knowledge until they fail, and learn why they failed: "making a wrong decision and subsequently failing is also being empowered and facilitates learning something, compared to being forced to succeed, but not really learning anything" (Hyltoft, 2010).

Hyltoft's essay, and his work, is encouraging and what I learned from him through reading and then visiting a school in Denmark helped correct some of the mistakes I made with my first attempt at an edu-LARP: Star Seekers.

Star Seekers

Filled with vim and vigor to transform education using live action role-playing, I started to test my first LARP with a class of 21 sixth-graders for roughly 60 minutes a day, a few days a week for about a month. Less than $200 was spent on materials, about a quarter of which was spent on photocopying colored cardstock for group handouts.

The teacher we were working with emphasized the need to differentiate problems within the same subject, say, fractions, with varying difficulty for different students. This played into Starship Valkyrie easily, since that LARP works with a crew operating different ship sections. Each student rotated between the bridge, engineering, stardusters (single-pilot spaceships without hyperspace capability), and science and observation. The class was divided into four color-coded sections based on the teacher's recommendations for group dynamics and level of difficulty for their assignments. We gave each student a strip of colored fabric to indicate their group, and a light blue sash and a call sign name, like Hawk or Falcon. They wrote their code name on the sash and wore it as a makeshift uniform, keeping it after the LARP finished. Costumes and props, even simple ones, often go a very long way in LARPs, especially for children.

Each section had tasks for the ship's mission: engineering had math problems that created power for the ship, observation used science to figure out puzzles, stardusters ran through a gauntlet of basic math flash cards, and the bridge guided the other three and corrected the problems from engineering. Ideally, the students would work together to complete the mission, and we'd assign more missions in subsequent classes.

The first trial failed. We underestimated the time it would take to move the student's desks into a new "four-section" configuration, give them sashes and codenames, and explain the LARP idea. These flaws were easily corrected. The biggest problem was an assumption that students would be relatively proficient in the problems we assigned, particularly those in math and engineering ones. When they couldn't do the problems, they couldn't power the ship's engines, and the narrative failed. Star Seekers wasn't introductory instruction—it was intended to be a fun way of reviewing what the students already knew. Unfortunately, we didn't check the math and science problems with the teacher to see if they were appropriate before we presented them in the LARP. Worse, we attached narrative progress too abstract, unrelated drill and kill worksheets—our version of the dreaded "chocolate covered broccoli." Lastly, we grossly ignored the importance of social status among this age group, and giving the characters on the bridge authority over other students proved problematic.

But we learned, reiterated, and improved.

We set up each group to have a rotating leader; every time they would switch to a different section, which happened about every 10 minutes, they had a new group leader. This way each section only had one person to address. We readjusted the difficulty of the problems, and encouraged the group on the bridge to help engineering if they needed it. This worked well, as students proficient in the math would help those who weren't. They did this because they wanted the power boosts correct answers generated. We also gave the students more agency, which is a LARP term for the ability of your character to influence the narrative. For example, students could choose to increase shields or engine power, or maneuver to shoot an incoming asteroid or rescue someone in an escape pod. We added flashier props, and better graphics for the science problems. In the last class, we activated a video conference chat so the students could negotiate with an alien (played by an actor who donated his time to us) in real time. Although this was a highlight for the class, more students were interested in talking to the alien through the camera than the math problems.

After each run, we tried to assess results with help from the teacher. We estimated we reached 80% of the class at any one time; there were always a few who weren't participating or acted disruptive. They did learn some new material, but since this wasn't the goal, it was incidental. Some students improved on some tasks, but I believe the best result was that the teacher could tell which lessons she would need to review or not, and for which students. She had a better understanding of the class's proficiency for all the subjects we addressed, which she could work on before testing. Though Star Seekers was far from perfect, it still indicated to me that the concept of educational LARP is sound.

Scan the QR code or visit **youtu.be/254TAJ8cxZs** to check out a YouTube video of Star Seekers including student testimonials and examples of play.

Hit Seekers

I view edu-LARPs like tabletop role-playing games, where the lesson is the module or printed adventure, the teacher is the game master, and the students are the players. Most gamemasters customize and hack the published scenarios, or write their own to fit their players' wants and needs. It's easier to change words on a computer than ink on paper or, if the teacher isn't a programmer, coded software.

For this edu-LARP with high school students, the class was separated into groups. Each group representing a music company with $1 million as starting capital. They needed to use this imaginary money to sign fictional artists, attach them to a fictional producer, and book them into a fictional recording studio to make an album. Each artist, producer, and studio had different costs, time to record, percentage take of royalties, and quality they could add to each album. The better the album, the more fans an artist brought to the table, the more sales were made, and the more money was earned. The goal of each group was to net the highest profit. To properly make an album, the students needed to do the accounting (addition and subtraction) for the artist, producer, and studio. They also had a daily overhead based on how many people were in their group.

The game lasted a few months, and, once it started, students could sign artists any time they were in class. Once the album was complete, I would run the numbers through a simple formula and generate a gross revenue and net profit for each company. I reported this information on Twitter, which the students could follow. Once a week, I would come to class to check on the teacher and students, and offer goodies: they could exchange bonus points that came with each album release for snacks or save them for gift cards at the end of the year. Bonus points went to the company, not to individuals, so they would have to manage each person's hunger—an exercise in deferred gratification. For the last week of the game, companies could gain extra sales if they booked their artists into clubs, and to do that they had to figure out how many tickets they could sell in each club by finding the area of, say, the Rhomboid Room, or a round arena with a stage in the middle (compute area of two circles, subtract smaller from larger).

Hit Seekers also had the problem of being a review; other than the new concepts of overhead and royalties, the math was earned addition, subtraction, percentages, and basic algebra and geometry. In the first lessons we gave each company an accounting ledger book (a prop instead of a costume) to record their finances. One group was unresponsive. I checked on them and realized one student could not correctly read a six-figure number. They weren't sure if it was one million, six hundred thousand or sixteen-thousand—it was one hundred sixty thousand. Again, we based the mechanics of the game on assumed skill proficiency. When students lacked that proficiency, the game stopped. Fortunately, with help from their teammates, and myself, they were all able to operate slightly above the minimum. While this wasn't the last edu-LARP I made that focused on review, it is now my least-favorite option, especially when I'm unfamiliar with each student and his or her competency solving the problems needed to tell a story.

 Scan the QR codes (or visit **youtu.be/yk-ksF6L0LE and youtu. be/YjDVhmSeAuo**) to view two short videos from Hit Seekers.

 Download a free alpha version of Hit Seekers at **drivethrurpg.com** or by scanning the QR code.

Ancient Mesopotamia

Building an edu-LARP around a theme was a model I had viewed at a private school in Denmark. In this system, the LARP is one week, one theme, for all classes. For example, one week the students were asked to pretend they were staff on a cruise ship, and had to keep their passengers happy while on the journey. Another theme featured a police procedural like the show *CSI,* with students acting as police officers tracking a serial killer. Each week, all teachers worked together to attach their lesson plans to the same theme. For example, the killer leaves clues from classic literature that the officers need to read to create a profile, and one victim's body was dissolved in acid, so a chemistry expert, a.k.a. the science teacher, is called in as a consultant.

For the Ancient Mesopotamia edu-LARP the teachers delivered a traditional lecture presentation on Mesopotamian history and culture to get the students familiarized with the setting. We then gave students their characters, as a governor, astrologer, merchant, or priest from one of four ancient cities: Sippar, Borsippa, Dilbat, or Kish. Each character had two axes of potential alliances: with their role or their home city. We gave each character three goals, like host the biggest religious festival in the city, plus three academic goals for the player, which involved research and thought questions that could be easily turned into an assignment. The citizens of Dilbat all had a secret: they were time-travelers sent to study ancient Mesopotamia, and would be making a report at the end of the LARP. We did this to make things more challenging for the advanced students, and to provide another mode of instruction on the material, this time from peers.

Each day of the week had three basic periods, which matched the regular class structure at the school: one we called a "fishbowl," when the characters could mingle in a freeform situation as their characters—trading goods, planning festivals, or moving armies on a map against aggressors to the empire. During the other two periods, one role would lead the others on a specific module activity, which they prepared in a prior class. The activities were:

> **A market bazaar** where the merchants, used clay and small pencils to create symbols for trade goods like fish, grain, and cloth, and learned about changing market value of commodities (see Figure 2.1).

> **Fortune telling** with the astrologers, who used a paper star wheel we created using the constellations and base-60 number system of the Babylonians.

> **A courtroom** run by the governors under the Code of Hammurabi, with cases we introduced for them to adjudicate. Other players would pretend to be the litigants, not their own characters.

> **Presentation of the "Epic of Gilgamesh"**, which the students turned into a call and response play with the other students.

By almost all accounts, this run went very well. We saw emergent gameplay when one character was caught trying to steal items in the bazaar. I suggested he go on trial the next day for the governor's activity. That player went home and planned his defense, presenting a solid, yet ultimately unsuccessful, explanation. We also witnessed some intrinsic motivation, as one student researched the role of priests in this era. The next day, he delivered an impromptu presentation to the teachers that the priests' income was too low, that they had many duties in that time and should get a higher daily income. The teachers, playing the Judges of Babylon, agreed. Within seconds, I was handing out the additional income to all the priests (see Figure 2.2). Could a video game alter that parameter so easily and quickly?

It also happens that one very cunning student, playing a governor with armies, arranged a coup d'état, overthrowing the Judges of Babylon, a.k.a., the teachers.

CHARACTER SHEET from Ancient Mesopotamia

NAME: **Gadatas**   GROUP: **Merchant**

CITY-STATE: **Kish**   INCOME: **2 Gur of Fish, 1 Gur of Meat**

You are a merchant who lives in the city-state of Kish in the land of Mesopotamia. Kish is about seven miles east of the holy city of Babylon, where Hammurabi, a fair and just King, reigns. Kish and Babylon, along with the cities of Sippar, Borsippa, and Dilbat make up the Babylonian Kingdom. If you make honest and profitable trades, you could be one of the city's wealthiest citizens one day.

Character Goals

These are goals for your character. Have fun with them.

1. **You want to sell all your goods in exchange for silver shekels. This will help you start your new import business in Kish.**

2. **You are trying to build a reputation as being the most fair of any merchant. The written contract is the foundation of commerce in Babylonia. Your contracts should be easily readable by others. That means making sure that everyone gets a fair deal, not just you.**

3. **You want to build a warehouse in Kish. This requires 1 Timber and 1 Stone. But the more you get, the bigger a warehouse you can build. If you could get 5 Timber and 5 Stone, your warehouse would be HUGE!**

Academic Goals

What are some of the ways people actually traded goods in Ancient Mesopotamia? We know they didn't have cars and planes, so how did they get their goods from place to place?

Why do you think cuneiform—writing—developed? What are the strengths and weaknesses of writing with these symbols? Can you think of an easier way to write things down that everyone can use?

Would you rather make a deal with a handshake or a written contract? Why?

Figure 2.1. Character sheet for Ancient Mesopotamia LARP.

Figure 2.2. Student after negotiating new income
during Mesopotamia LARP.

Panicked at first, the classroom teachers rolled with it, and let them rule (not the
actual class, but the fictional LARP). In this iteration, they allowed characters to
petition the government for things like extra income. As soon as the new gover-
nors took power, the former Judges of Babylon began petitioning them, as did the
other students. The usurpers learned very quickly that running a government is
far more difficult than overthrowing one.

Would this be possible outside of a live action role-playing experience, where the
unexpected is refused by a computer rather than handled by an adaptable human
being? A teacher's ability to improvise is crucial in the classroom, and more so in
edu-LARPs. While this may seem difficult to some teachers, improvisation is what,
I believe, ensures that LARPing will always be a superior method of instruction
than any locked curricula, whether locked in printed pages or locked in code.

Tips, Tricks, Techniques, and Expectations

Hopefully I made the obvious errors so you won't have to. Following are some
things I've learned after five years of designing and running edu-LARPs. I'm still
learning, and hope I'll get the opportunity to continue learning for the rest of my
life. Hopefully I made the obvious errors so you won't have to. None of these define
the only pathway for educational live action role-playing, but serve as helpful
guidelines.

Use Narrative

I believe someone has a better shot remembering the quadratic formula because they used it at a dramatic moment to save a spaceship from plunging into the sun than if they got it right on a test. Stories connect unmoored facts to emotional foundations. Even a simple patina of fiction can change a traditional class: Østerskov Efterskole's police procedural LARP featured a "normal" chemistry lecture about acids and bases. But pretend the students are cops trying to catch a killer and the teacher is a consultant, and the knowledge becomes important—possibly more vital than remembering it for a test or course grade. Stories are powerful, and often stay with us throughout our lives.

Avoid Trivia

In Gamedesk's educational program, *Ancient Inventions*, students are asked trivia questions about a historical culture. If correct, students receive pieces to build an ancient invention, like a shaduf (lever for moving water). But why impose a barrier to doing something cool, like building a lever with Popsicle sticks? I revised the game so participants would get to build the machine first, then learn about the history and culture surrounding the device. Trivia is often the easiest way of presenting information, but I don't think it leads to a deep understanding—the knowledge is trivial and not relevant to what students want to do.

Don't Be Clever

Education should not be about showing off how smart you are. When designing edu-LARPs, what you think is neat might be dull dry toast to your students. Running games should not pit your brain against theirs; it's not that kind of competition. Let students have the thrill of discovery, encourage their own passion to learn more over inserting what you think is interesting. LARP gives people a heuristic chance to create their own story. Encourage them.

Allow for Character Failure

Allowing students to fail, learn from their mistakes, and try again is vital to learning. Video games inherently do this, LARPs need to as well. The mask of role-playing allows the character to fail, which isn't the same as the player. It's okay if students try new things that don't work. Give them the freedom to lose, ensure they know why they failed, and give them the chance to try again. In traditional teaching, wrong answers on homework and tests lead to lower grades and disenchantment with the subject. LARPs and games should allow students to learn from failures. For example, in *Ancient Inventions* we asked students to make the machine first and after their first attempt we explained the math and science behind it. Then we gave them the chance to improve their construct.

Break Bottlenecks

In traditional learning, one teacher or one textbook has all the answers, and student comprehension hinges on their ability to receive a strong signal through all the noise of modern schooling and, sometimes, inefficient teachers or worksheets. With edu-LARPs, there can be multiple sources of knowledge, including peer-to-peer learning. You can save time by explaining how to do something to one student, and they'll explain it to the others.

Manage Chaos

In most edu-LARPs, the classroom gets loud, and the energy rises. Students might be yelling, running around, and waving their arms. In most instances, this is good thing. If students remain focused most of the time, noise and activity are indicators of learning. However, unless you have administrative support and understanding, especially from classes adjacent to yours, plus the ability to rein in the group, chaos can be disruptive. There's a balance all teachers need to reach between a riot and total silence—both can be unproductive.

Competition Can Be Your Ally

Harnessing the competitive desire can be a strong motivator for learning. Most LARPs group characters into competing factions, though sometimes there are spies or traitors for one side or another. Students accept loss if the system is fair, they learned the reason for their failure, and they can play again.

Don't Assume

This is an obvious mantra for life, but as you probably noticed from my case studies, a critical error was assuming students already knew the material they needed to play the LARP. Even if you're the class teacher, students might have forgotten material you've already presented to them. Related to this, don't predict student performance, especially for the narrative. Like teaching in general, you have to be ready for anything. The show must go on; the narrative must keep rolling unless there is an emergency. In hindsight, when our first Star Seekers crew failed at their math problems, we should have switched groups, asked others to help them, or launched into a group training course on that material.

Integrate Topics

One of the joys designing edu-LARPs is bringing in material from multiple subjects. For me, it is easier to include history with science, a la The Great Phlogiston Debate, than separating them into individual topics, especially when different teachers are asynchronous with their lessons. Whenever possible, collaborate with other teachers so their lessons reinforce or assist the edu-LARP.

Have Fun in Your Role

Teachers should also have a character to role-play. This allows you to model enthusiasm and encourage others to join. It also gives you two avenues of engagement and discipline: that of the character and that of the teacher (if needed for discipline). Moreover, being in the role-play pool with your students affords a unique perspective to see the lesson through your students' eyes. You can enjoy the mystery and experience as much as they do, since you won't know how the narrative ends, which might help if you teach year after year.

Provide a Role or Duty for Non-Participants

Some students are unwilling or unable to participate in the LARP, for whatever reason. Often a LARP requires detailed accounting or tracking, and in the frenzy of role-playing, another set of eyes could prove invaluable.

Appendix

Sample Introduction to Live Action Role-Playing

Ideally, using live action role-playing for education will prompt a resurgence in curiosity, attention, and empowerment. This appendix provides a sample introduction to LARPS to get started.

1. Introduction: What is a LARP?

This should take 10 minutes at most. Teachers should explain that LARP stands for "live action role-playing" Some of the students might be familiar with the concept, or have participated in a LARP. Tell them it's like playing cops and robbers, or tea parties with stuffed animals, or any kind of acting without a script or camera, where the audience is each other and no one else. If students react poorly, say it's an acting game like the Model United Nations, or a historical simulation. It's like *World of Warcraft*, but acted out in the classroom instead of played on a computer.

Tell the students they will each have a character they will pretend to be. Explain that the characters we play (and teachers will be characters as well) are not the people they actually are! If a character is angry with you, that person isn't angry with you as a person. This is play-pretend.

2. LARP Exercise

Explain that you're going to do a, very short, role-playing exercise, just to get the hang of it. Photocopy and randomly hand out the character strips listed in the next section, one to each student (and take one for yourselves). Explain that this is their character role. Give them two minutes to read it over, then look around, yell "game on!" and let them go. After 10 minutes, the game is over. Encourage students to be creative with their interpretation of the character sheets, even if the character is unfamiliar.

3. Review Exercise and Debrief

Explain that they pretended to be someone else. Obviously, no one was actually that character. The same thing happens in LARPs: they will all have a character to play, to interact together in an imaginary world based on real historical facts. Students should research their characters so they can pretend to be them. They can continue to do this out of school, during breaks, or during prep time.

Emphasize that there isn't a right or wrong way to play your character. If they fail, or don't complete their goals, or screw up—that's fine. It's just a play pretend character. You decide what they are like based on the information you get, but try to achieve your goals.

Characters for Live Action Role-Playing Exercise

Photocopy the following character strips and hand out randomly to players, including teachers. *Do not let anyone trade.* They can research the person quickly, before the exercise begins. Feel free to create your own characters following this model:

1. **One sentence on who they are.**

2. **Name one person they know; this can be a friend or enemy.**

3. **One goal, piece of knowledge, or thing they want to do.**

You are Harry Potter, a young wizard of the Hogwarts School of Witchcraft and Wizardry.

You know Hermione.

You think someone here has a magical artifact. You don't have a wand.

You are Hermione Granger, a witch at the Hogwarts School of Witchcraft and Wizardry.

You know Harry Potter.

You think someone here has a magical artifact. You don't have a wand.

You are Frodo Baggins, a hobbit.

You know Gollum.

You have the One Ring but want to give it to anyone EXCEPT Gollum.

You are Gollum, a deranged creature.

You know Frodo Baggins.

You want to get the One Ring from Frodo.

You are Kanye West, a superstar hip hop artist.

You know Rhianna, Lady Gaga, and Justin Bieber.

You want to find someone else to make a record with you.

You are Rhianna, a superstar singer.

You know Kanye West, Lady Gaga, and Justin Bieber.

You want to get Kanye West to apologize for something he did wrong.

You are Lady Gaga, a superstar singer.

You know Kanye West, Rihanna, and Justin Bieber.

You want to protest the cruel treatment of animals.

You are Justin Bieber, a superstar singer.

You know Kanye West, Rihanna, and Lady Gaga.

You want to show you are nice and don't want to be prosecuted on assault charges.

You are Santa Claus, a jolly fellow that brings toys to kids.

You know everyone here when they tell you their name.

You want to make sure you know what each person wants for Christmas.

You are Cookie Monster, a hungry Muppet.

You don't know anyone here.

You want to find cookies and eat them.

References

Huizinga, J. (2016). *Homo Ludens: A Study of the Play Element in Culture*. Boston, MA: Beacon Press.

Hyltoft, M. (2010). *Four reasons why Edu-larp works*. Retrieved from thenoon.ru/files/documents/file_74d48f19a41a0db0c5fe0dcd15763464.pdf

Vanek, A. (2009). *Cooler Than You Think: Understanding Live Action Role-Playing.*

World Economic Forum. (2014) *A Day in the Life of a Refugee*. Retrieved from refugee-run.org/press/refugee- run-quotes- feedback.html

3

Game Creation as a Learning Activity for All Students

By KIP GLAZER

ISTE Standards for Students

3 Knowledge Constructor. Students critically curate a variety of resources using digital tools to construct knowledge, produce creative artifacts and make meaningful learning experiences for themselves and others.

5 Computational Thinker. Students develop and employ strategies for understanding and solving problems in ways that leverage the power of technological methods to develop and test solutions.

6 Creative Communicator. Stud ents communicate clearly and express themselves creatively for a variety of purposes using the platforms, tools, styles, formats and digital media appropriate to their goals.

In recent years, game-based learning has shown great promise in the field of education. With the implementation of Common Core State Standards (CCSS) and the accompanying technological advancement in education, teachers are seeking new ways to enhance the learning experience in their classrooms. As evidenced by the plethora of books, articles, and blogs published by organizations like the International Society for Technology in Education (ISTE), International Literacy Association (ILA), Society for Information Technology and Teacher Education (SITE), Edutopia, and MindShift, game-based learning is one of the ways educators are working to incorporate innovative teaching strategies into their classrooms to meet the demands of their profession.

Game studies and game-based learning have begun to experience prominence in recent years (Gee, 2007; Kafai, 2006; Malaby, 2007; Steinkuehler, 2006a), and if the recent successes of multiplayer games like *Minecraft* or augmented reality games such as *Pokemon GO* are any indication, games and game-based learning is here to stay. Even businesses now use the term *gamification* to describe using game mechanics to maximize the profitability of their businesses (Drell, 2014).

Why Game-Based Learning?

Despite the recent insurgence, interest in games for learning has waxed and waned over many decades. In the early 1980s, popular games like *The Oregon Trail* (1974) and *Where in the World is Carmen Sandiego?* (1985) offered simulations of history and science. Other games like *Reader Rabbit* (1986) or *Math Blaster* (1991) provided playful drill and practice of reading and math concepts (Edwards, 2012). The revival of interest in educational games seems to have appeared around 2004 with a growing recognition among researchers that massively multiplayer online games and game communities embodied powerful learning activities.

Earlier game studies focused on their impact on spatial abilities or the development of the learners' specific scholastic skills like reading and mathematics (Aguilera & Méndiz, 2003). In recent years, more and more scholars have focused on the impact of video games and gameplay on developing problem-solving, decision making, and collaboration skills (Aguilera & Méndiz, 2003; Squire, 2003). Game scholars have argued that in today's media-saturated society where most students are accustomed to information creation utilizing technological tools, the conventional pedagogy that focuses on a linear progression has become grossly inadequate (Gee, 2004, 2007; Selfe, Hawisher, & Ittersum 2007). To live in a modern, globally networked society, students must be given learning opportunities to become producers of new knowledge (Benkler, 2006; Black, 2008; Jenkins, 2006).

For many years, I have used games in my classroom as a teaching tool. I have always felt the interactive and interest-focused nature of games enhanced my instruction tremendously (see Figure 3.1). Games in the classroom help teachers to connect with their students. Undoubtedly, my students have always loved to play and discuss games more so than any other instructional tools. Gameplay can also facilitate the development of critical skills like listening, speaking, collaboration, and leadership development. While playing well-designed video or digital games, students frequently produce, consume, remix, and critique all sorts of media. By negotiating the rules and structure of games, students can learn to reside successfully in a world that isn't of their creation—one of the main goals of public education. I have personally witnessed my students become interested and engaged in learning simply because we were playing games in the classroom.

Figure 3.1. *Literary Clue: A Game of Whodunit?* A game that matches literary theme to authors.

Game Players as Game Creators

While there are amazing benefits of playing sophisticated games created by others, gameplay limits the players to being passive participants of the learning activity since all the information, major structure, and rules are determined by the creators of the game. By allowing the students to create the games to be played, teachers can create a fully situated learning environment (Greeno, 2006; Martinez & Stager, 2013). Since the students must actively participate in the knowledge creation process, game creation naturally allows students to become in charge of their own learning. Game creation as a pedagogical strategy contains many characteristics of Papert's constructionist model (Papert & Harel, 1991). According to Papert, learning activities focused on concrete knowledge were just as important as developing abstract thoughts (Ackermann, 2001; Kafai, 2006b). Learning was both situated and pragmatic; therefore, artifact construction was not only useful but also imperative (Papert & Harel, 1991). Furthermore, game creation extends the notion of motivation for learning (Gee, 2007; Kafai, 2006a; Papert & Harel, 1991). Since it allows them more control over their environment, learners can gain the motivational benefits based on the dimensions of self-identification (Klimmt, Hefner, & Vorderer, 2009). Researchers have shown players are highly motivated while playing video games (Malone & Lepper, 1987). However, there is frequently a gap between what's enjoyable for players and what the designers' intended for them to gain by playing (Wang, Shen, & Ritterfeld, 2009). Game creation successfully closes an enjoyment gap that often impedes learner motivation. Since the students create the game they want to play, the game creation process promotes strong learner agency among students (Bandura, 2002). Game creation, therefore, is a viable pedagogical strategy for all teachers.

Implementing Game Creation as an Instructional Strategy

For many years, I successfully used game creation as an instructional strategy with my English Language Learners (ELL) who spoke little or no English as well as my Advanced English literature class who were receiving college credit to meet the particular instructional objectives appropriate for their skill levels.

If you have never tried this strategy, I would start doing so as a review activity for finals. I typically had my students work in pairs or groups to create the game, but it can work for individual students depending on your class size. Before starting, here are some things to consider.

Opportunity Cost

Consider how much time you can spend in your classroom to facilitate the creation process. While your primary focus is for them to learn important concepts while creating the game, many students tend to focus on the final product. Enlisting help from others outside of the class to create the most polished can minimize loses the benefits of learning through creation within set parameters. To avoid this you can have students create the game in class. However, that's not always possible or feasible. One way to compromise is to have the groups create a detailed plan that includes the content the groups or individual intend to cover, type of game mechanics, and who is responsible for what task.

Technology

Over the years, I used digital tools like Kodu©, Construct2, or GameMaker©with my students. Obviously, a *Jeopardy*-style review game planned using index cards moved to a digital format can achieve the same goal and won't take much effort to create. However, I found having the students make analog games (i.e., board games or card games) tends to invite more participation in both the game creation and play testing phases. We all need to remember that paper and pencil in the hands of skilled teachers can be the most powerful instructional technology tool.

Content

Certain content simply won't be appropriate for game creation. For instance, I saw a casino game using *Moby Dick* with a whale chasing a captain of a boat. The goal

Figure 3.2. *Educopoly!* A class rules review game

Figure 3.3a. Playtesting *Educopoly!*

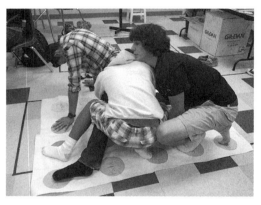

Figure 3.3b. Playtesting *LitTwister!*

of the game was to kill the whale. That type of game mechanic will not achieve the goal of teaching the content. For a review game, it's better to use critical terms like important literary terms or simple processes like chemical reactions or immune system responses (see Figure 3.2). Students often don't like the repetitive process of memorizing certain terms or processes, but by having them create a game, students can be exposed to such concepts multiple times without the same feelings of monotony.

You should allow your students to play the games that they created for a chance to review and experience the game as players (see Figures 3.3a and 3.3b). However, you should always remember that even when the game isn't as aesthetically pleasing or sophisticated, the students who created it had to interact with the content multiple times to create the final product.

Appendix

Lesson Plan

The following is a lesson plan I have created and used over the years. While the rubrics are included, you don't need to use them since they can be adapted to meet the student and teacher needs.

May the Best Game Win!

The objective of your game is to "teach" a critical concept. After the playing testing session, the creators of the game chosen by the teacher and voted by their peers will receive extra credit on their final. If there is a dispute as to which game is the best teaching or review tool, the teacher always has final say.

Step 1: Gather the content such as literary terms, mathematical equations, or chemical elements.

Step 2: Put your students in groups. I recommend allowing them to choose their own group since this activity requires a high level of interaction.

Step 3: Have the group create a planning document that answers the following questions:

> What type of game do they plan to create?
>
> Why do they think that particular game will be the most useful in teaching and reviewing the concepts?
>
> Who will be responsible for which elements of the game?

Step 4: Have them share the document with another group to get feedback. The reviewers should focus on the following questions when sharing feedback:

> Is the game practical and reasonable for review?
>
> Do you think the team has enough time to complete the task, for example, build a playable game? If not, what can they change?
>
> Do you think the task seems to be equally divided?
>
> Is the document detailed enough for anyone to be able to use to create their own game?

Step 5: Create a review game.

Sample Planning Document Rubric					
CATEGORY	DID NOT COMPLETE THE TASK (0)	DID NOT MEET THE STANDARDS	MET THE STANDARDS	EXCEEDED THE STANDARDS	SCORE
Appropriateness and completeness of the plan	The group did not complete the task (0).	The group created an incomplete plan for a game that doesn't seem to cover the necessary content for a final review. (1-14).	The group created a solid plan for a game that seems to have enough details for a final review. (15-17).	The group created a detailed plan for a game that has more than enough details for a successful review. (18-20).	/20
Grammar and Syntax.		There are too many errors (1-2).	There are a few errors, but they did not obscure the meaning of the text (3).	There are few errors, and the writing shows a level of competency (4-5)	/5
TOTAL	/25				

Step 6: Play test the games. On the play testing day, set up different stations. One person from the original creators stays at the table to explain how to play the game and run the game. The rest go and play as many games as they can.

Step 7: Write a reflection on what you learned from playing the games.

Playtest Rubric					
CATEGORY	DID NOT COMPLETE THE TASK (0)	DID NOT MEET THE STANDARDS	MET THE STANDARDS	EXCEEDED THE STANDARDS	SCORE
Appropriateness and completeness of the game	The group did not complete the task (0).	The game did not provide enough details and content. (1-14).	The game provided enough details and content. (15-17).	The game provided enough details and content. I would recommend it as the tool for a review (18-20).	/30
TOTAL	/30				

References

Ackermann, E. (2001). Piaget's constructivism, Papert's constructionism: What's the difference? Retrieved from http://learning.media.mit.edu/content/publications/EA.Piaget%20_%20Papert.pdf

Aguilera, M. D., & Méndiz, A. (2003). Video games and education. *Computers in Entertainment, 1*(1), 10. doi:10.1145/950566.950583

Bandura, A. (2002). Social cognitive theory in cultural context. *Applied Psychology: An International Review, 51*(2), 269-290. doi:10.1111/1464-0597.00092

Benkler, Y. (2006). *The Wealth of Networks.* New Haven, CT: Yale University Press.

Black, R. W. (2008). *Adolescents and online fan fiction.* New York, NY: Peter Lang.

Drell, L. (2014). Let the gamification begin. *Marketing Health Services,* 24-27. Retrieved from https://www.ama.org/

Edwards, B. (2012). 10 educational PC games of the 1980s. Retrieved from http://www.pcmag.com/slideshow/story/293124/10-educational-pc-games-of-the-1980s

Gee, J. P. (2004). *Situated language and learning: a critique of traditional schooling.* New York, NY: Routledge.

Gee, J. P. (2007). *What video games have to teach us about learning and literacy* (2nd ed.). New York, NY: Palgrave Macmillan.

Greeno, J. (2006a). Learning in activity. In K. Sawyer (Ed.), *The Cambridge handbook of the learning sciences,* 79-96. New York, NY: Cambridge University Press.

Jenkins, H. (2006b). *Convergence culture: where old and new media collide.* Retrieved from www.nypress.org

Kafai, Y. (2006). Constructionism. In R. K. Sawyer (Ed.), *The Cambridge handbook of the learning sciences,* 35-46. New York, NY: Cambridge University Press.

Kafai, Y. (2006). Playing and making games for learning: Instructionist and constructionist perspectives for game studies. *Games and Culture, 1*(1), 36-40. doi:10.1177/1555412005281767

Klimmt, C., Hefner, D., & Vorderer, P. (2009). The video game experience as "true" identification: A theory of enjoyable alterations of players' self-perception. *Communication Theory, 19*(4), 351-373. doi:10.1111/j.1468-2885.2009.01347.x

Malaby, T. M. (2007). Beyond play: A new approach to games. *Games and Culture, 2*(2), 95-113. doi:10.1177/1555412007299434

Malone, T. W., & Lepper, M. R. (1987). Making learning fun: A taxonomy of intrinsic motivations for learning. In R. Snow, & M. J. Farr (Eds.), *Aptitude, learning, and instruction* (Vol. 3): *Conative and affective process analyses.* Hillsdale, NJ: Lawrence Erlbaum Associates.

Martinez, S. L., & Stager, G. (2013). *Invent to learn: Making, tinkering, and engineering in the classroom.* Retrieved from www.InventToLearn.com

Papert, S., & Harel, I. (1991). Situating constructionism. In *Constructionism.* Retrieved from http://www.papert.org/articles/SituatingConstructionism.html

Selfe, C., Hawisher, G., Ittersum, D. (Eds.) (2007). Gaming lives in the twenty-first century: literate connections. New York: Palgrave Macmillan.

Squire, K. (2003). Video games in education. *International Journal of Intelligent Games & Simulation, 2*(1), 49-62. Retrieved from http://website.education.wisc.edu/~kdsquire/tenure-files/39-squire-IJIS.pdf

Steinkuehler, C. A. (2006). Why game (culture) studies now? *Games and Culture, 1*(1), 97-102. doi:10.1177/1555412005281911

Wang, H., Shen, C. & Ritterfeld, U. (2009). Enjoyment of digital games: What makes them "seriously" fun? In U.Ritterfeld, M.Cody & P.Vorderer (Eds.), *Serious Games: Mechanisms and Effects.* New York, NY: Routledge.

4

Gamifying Culinary Arts

By TISHA RICHMOND

1 Empowered Learner. Students leverage technology to take an active role in choosing, achieving and demonstrating competency in their learning goals, informed by the learning sciences.

3 Knowledge Constructor. Students critically curate a variety of resources using digital tools to construct knowledge, produce creative artifacts and make meaningful learning experiences for themselves and others.

5 Computational Thinker. Students develop and employ strategies for understanding and solving problems in ways that leverage the power of technological methods to develop and test solutions.

I have always loved incorporating game-based elements and principles into my culinary arts classes. There is an energy and excitement created when students engage in playing a game. Creating class competitions that mimic *Chopped* or *Cupcake Wars* allows students to implement the skills they've learned to create something unique and amazing. Adding components like "mystery baskets" and surprise ingredients produces an element of surprise and challenge that encourages problem-solving and collaboration among students. Inviting teachers, staff, and administrators into the classroom as judges encourages students to step up their game and show off their skills. Often students that shine in my class may struggle in their core subjects, so giving them the opportunity to share their strengths with a broader audience is vitally important.

Inspiration

Two years ago, I was inspired by *Explore Like a Pirate* (2015) author, Michael Matera, at a conference called Miami Device where he led a session on game-inspired course design. I was blown away by his gamified approach to education and knew I had to learn more. It was then I began transforming my classroom from one that incorporated games and competitions occasionally to one built entirely around a game. It all started with inspiration. I watched a lot of television reality shows like *MasterChef, The Great Food Truck Race*, and *The Amazing Race*. I started rethinking the way I teach my classes and considering how I could overlay a gamified framework to make learning come alive for my students.

Theme

The biggest challenge for me was finding where to start. Though I loved the idea of creating a gamified learning environment, I wasn't sure how to set it up. Matera recommended I begin by choosing a theme, and then everything else would start to fall into place. I began pulling ideas from the shows that were inspiring me, and I decided on *MasterChef* as a theme for my culinary arts gamified classroom (see Figure 4.1).

Story

To begin developing my game I created a story from my theme that included setting, character, and action.

Aspiring chefs embark on an adventure where they will explore the world of culinary arts in a quest to be MasterChef. There are opportunities to earn badges individually and as a team. These badges give students experience points (XP) that will unlock special privileges and opportunities for each student and their team, moving them closer to becoming MasterChef.

Badges

The overall goal of the game is to become MasterChef for each unit and ultimately earn three Michelin Stars before the end of the semester. Becoming MasterChef holds special privileges. If students earn MasterChef status (4,000 XP)

MasterChef

STORY:
THEME
MasterChef

SETTING
MasterChef Kitchen

CHARACTERS
Aspiring Chefs

ACTION
Culinary Missions
Team Challenges
Adventure Quest
Mini Games

LEVELS:
Line Cook   1000 XP
  Notecard on test

Sous Chef   2000 XP
  Test with partner

MasterChef   4000 XP
  Exempt from test
  Free cooking day
  Michelin Star

GOAL:
Students are on a quest each unit to become MasterChef and ultimately earn 3 Michelin Stars before the end of the semester.

BADGES:
Each unit students can earn badges worth varying amounts of XP that will move them closer to becoming MasterChef.

TEAM BADGES:
Labs & Challenges

INDIVIDUAL BADGES:
Culinary Missions, Mini Games, Adventure Quest

ITEMS:
Items are earned when students demonstrate extraordinary employability skills, mise en place, and sanitation.

- Extra day to turn in Culinary Missions
- Free mix-in ingredient
- Choose own recipe
- 5-minute time advantage in challenges
- Choice of music
- 5 minutes of help from teacher during challenge

UNLOCKING ACHIEVEMENTS:
A Michelin Star is earned each time a student reaches MasterChef status.

Figure 4.1. Syllabus for gamified culinary arts program.

by the end of the unit, they are exempt from the unit test. Yes, you heard me correctly—students don't have to take the test! My aspiring chefs have can earn badges with varying amounts of XP throughout each unit by demonstrating their understanding of the unit's essential questions. The test shows me they understand the essential questions, and earning exemption shows they've gone above and beyond to become "masters." Every student who has ever earned MasterChef status has proven they've mastered the content.

The badges in my class are tangible. I design badges the size of baseball cards using Apple Pages. I print them out in color and laminate them. As students earn badges, they keep them in clear baseball card sleeves that they keep in their binders. This system was recommended to me by Michael Matera and has worked extremely well. Students are accountable for holding onto their badges that are turned in at the end of the unit to determine what level they've reached (see Table 4.1).

Level Requirements		
LEVEL	XP REQUIRED TO REACH	REWARD UNLOCKED
Apprentice	1,000	Use a 3x5 card on unit test
Sous Chef	2,000	Work with another Sous Chef on test
Master Chef	4,000	Exempt from test, free cooking day, and Michelin Star

Table 4.1. Level requirements for playing MasterChef.

Badges can be earned in the following ways:

Missions

I launch three missions per unit that are tied to the unit's essential questions and require students to demonstrate their understanding in a creative way that goes above and beyond what we are doing in class. I don't give extra time in class for these missions. However, if students are finished with the classroom activities with time to spare, they can work on these missions with the time remaining. I'm always blown away by what students can demonstrate when you allow them to tap into their creativity! Most often they go far above what I would expect and they are not even being graded. These missions are worth 1,000 XP and are the best way to reach Masterchef status by the end of the unit.

Product Quality Badges

Teams can earn product quality badges by producing finished products in their culinary labs that exceed my expectations. I tell them that if they demonstrate their understanding of the methods so well that I would actually pay for their finished product if it was served in a bakery or a restaurant, they will receive a badge. This collaboration at its finest. It's inspiring to watch teams come together to create something phenomenal.

Mini Challenges

Within units, I will often have mini challenges that will give students the opportunity to earn varying numbers of XP. Mini challenges include review games like *Kahoot*, *Quizlet Live*, and timed challenges where students must create something within a specific time frame. These challenges add excitement and are an excellent opportunity for students to review content and move up in the game.

MasterChef Challenges

At the end of each unit students compete in a MasterChef challenge. In these challenges, I give teams the formula (ingredients and measurements) for a recipe that they learned in the unit, and they have to work together as a team to prepare it without the recipe instructions. They then make the recipe their own by adding something original. Creations are judged on taste, texture, appearance, and overall creativity. For example, in the pie and pastry unit, students have to make a pie crust without the recipe instructions and use it to create something amazing. I supply a variety of ingredients they can use for their creation. I send an email out to staff inviting them to judge the challenge. I create a judging panel and teams present their dish to the panel, to be judged as they would in the *MasterChef* television show. It's remarkable to see how much these challenges empower students to take their learning to another level by demonstrating what they know in a creative way. Having other staff members come in to judge the dishes definitely takes the challenge to another level.

Michelin Stars

When students reach MasterChef status by earning 4,000 XP, they earn a Michelin Star. This Michelin Star unlocks special privileges within the unit and a special status within the class. Ultimately, students are on a quest to earn three Michelin Stars before the end of the unit. This is the ultimate level to be earned, and their picture will forever be on the Michelin Star wall in my room. They also earn special recognition which isn't revealed until the end.

Items

As a career and technical education teacher, employability skills are very important. I keep track of the progress in employability throughout each unit. Students demonstrating extraordinary employability skills throughout the unit have the opportunity to earn items that unlock special privileges in class. Some items they can earn are: free mix-in ingredient, double your recipe, exemption from cleaning for a day, and free trip to the coffee bar. These items are printed and kept like the badges until students are ready to redeem them. Students love earning them and these privileges motivate them to continually strive to be the best "employee" they can be.

I'm a Believer

After two years of transforming my classes to a gamified model, I could never go back to how I taught my culinary classes before. The degree of collaboration, problem solving, and creativity that happens daily in my gamified classroom is astonishing. Students are more motivated to learn now than I've ever witnessed before and are doing more than what is required to earn MasterChef status. Learning has come alive in a way that I never imagined possible. Students are immersed and invested in the learning environment since they are given voice and choice in how they demonstrate their learning.

In my 16 years of teaching, I've never had more fun! I find inspiration all around me and am always thinking of new ideas to incorporate into my classroom. Students love to offer suggestions and ideas as well, keeping the game evolving. The beauty of gamifying is you can truly make it your own and you don't have to have it all figured out from the beginning. Let the game evolve, allowing for twists and turns to keep the lessons exciting and to meet the needs of all your learners. A gamification framework can truly be applied to any content or grade level. Find your inspiration and set your gamified class in motion!

References

Matera, M. (2015) *Explore like a Pirate: Gamification and game inspired course design to engage, enrich, and elevate your learners.* Dave Burgess Consulting, Inc.

5

Game On!

> How a Non-Gamer Learned to Gamify Her Classroom

By CARRIE BAUGHCUM

ISTE Standards for Students

1 Empowered Learner. Students leverage technology to take an active role in choosing, achieving and demonstrating competency in their learning goals, informed by the learning sciences.

3 Knowledge Constructor. Students critically curate a variety of resources using digital tools to construct knowledge, produce creative artifacts and make meaningful learning experiences for themselves and others.

5 Computational Thinker. Students develop and employ strategies for understanding and solving problems in ways that leverage the power of technological methods to develop and test solutions.

I vividly remember seeing the tweets about it—gamification. How it used the best part of games to bring out the best in your students. "Wow! This sounds seriously awesome. I have to try it," I remember thinking. Days and months passed. I saw more tweets and more comments about gamification, gamifying, XP, and how other teachers were using these strategies in education. It didn't take long before the idea of using the elements of games in your classroom to enhance learning became something I really wanted to try... someday. Someday when I had enough time, someday when I had the right students, someday.

Getting Started with Gamification

Months passed and the idea kept nagging at me. I decided to learn everything I could about gamification. I set out to learn how to build a gamified classroom, picking through sites to find stories and blog posts about gamified classrooms, accounts of all the fun the teachers and students were having, reflections about heightened engagement, and articles that taught me how gamification uses elements like mature make-believe play, play-based learning, and constant motivation to encourage learners to strive harder while enhancing and lessons that are already taking place in the classroom. I learned how gamification, improves accessibility in classrooms, increases the level of engagement, and requires students to develop, practice, and use teamwork, creativity, imagination, critical thinking, problem solving, flexibility, communication skills, and initiative. My research left me with lots of information but not the depth of learning and instruction I needed to feel confident gamifying my own classroom. Disappointed and too uncertain to try gamification myself, it continued to be a someday idea.

More time passed and this someday idea continued to nag at me, but now it started to whisper, "Try me. You'll love me. You know you want to try it!" In that moment, I decided it was time. It was time to take what I knew, trust what I had learned, have confidence in my skills as an educator, and jump in. It was time for me to bring gamification to my classroom. Completely terrified what I was about to try would be a disaster, I was also certain if it worked it would be incredible.

Excited and still completely unsure if I knew what I was doing, I started to plan my first game. Determined not to give up, I began to draw on what I knew about my students and how all successful planning in education starts. I started by thinking about what goals I had for my students. I most wanted my students to improve upon their skills and to be independent learners.

With these goals in mind, I started to ask myself questions like: What skills do my students need to master to achieve these goals? What skills do I want the points to reinforce? Most of all, I wanted the points my students earned to be based on observable skills and never grades or test scores.

Once the objectives and skills were clarified, it was time to decide on my game's theme. I considered the themes of some of my favorite games and finally settled on *Super Mario Bros*. My first classroom gamification had a simple game design—no tech, nothing flashy, just stars on the wall, dice, and paper points handed to students as XP. As simple as it was, this small step into gamification allowed me to start simple and really focus on the goals I set for my students. It left me feeling empowered, my students smiling, plus, it filled my classroom with pure fun!

The more we played, the more I learned about gamification. The earlier research I had done started to make more sense to me. The application of gamification elements like: rewards, quests, bonuses, competition, achievement levels, virtual currency to encourage collaboration, fun, focus, productivity, creativity, and meaningful choices—while encouraging the development of desired behaviors with immediate feedback—became clearer and easier to understand. The more we played, the more I saw how layering gamification over what I was already doing could impact my students engagement. Most of all, the more we played, the more comfortable I was adding these new elements to the game.

Taking It to the Next Level

With my first game under my belt, I was ready to design, create, and put into play my next game. My goals would stay the same, but with this game I was ready to diversify my game design skills. I would sit, close my eyes and imagine myself playing the game, seeing in my mind the parts and elements of games I loved to play and the parts that were my favorite. I began to ask myself questions like: What will students be able to do with their points? What would my game space look like? How will I display the leaderboard and show game progress? Will my game have tokens, power ups, badges, or other fun add-ons? With so many questions, I was certain my first game would certainly not be my last.

Three quarters and three games later, the school year came to an end, and my teaching, my classroom, and I would never be the same. It was game on and I was all in. I had a newfound confidence and gamification fearlessness. I would gamify my classroom again, but next year it would be a year-long game!

To sustain a full year of gamification, I wanted to use a movie theme (talk about endless possibilities) and decided on a Monopoly board format. That June I made it my personal goal to improve my gamification knowledge. I learned that the games I enjoyed most had certain things in common like well-designed graphics, easy to follow instructions, fun gameplay level ups, adventures, mysteries, and points to be earned and spent. Many games also included bonuses and the ability to connect with others as allies and resources.

The Gamification Process

After more game playing than I would like to admit, I started creating my game following this process, which has now become my step-by-step guide to gamifying my classroom:

1. Define Your Goals

What goals do you have for your students? What do you want to see from your students at the end of the school year? What do you want students to improve on?

2. Pick Your Theme

Think of a theme. It can be whatever you want it to be. It can match your personality and the personalities of your students. You might pick a theme based on a board or video game. Some themes I've tried are *Super Mario Bros.*, *Angry Birds Movieopoly*, *StarWarsopoly*, and *Star Wars*.

3. Define How Points Are Earned

My games use points to reinforce positive student skills and good behavior choices. I allowed my students two weeks to just earn points, with no game-play. Delaying the start of the game allowed my students to accrue points to use in the beginning of the game, or to to fall back on later in the game. I kept in mind the type of learners that are in my class. Some students need consistent and more frequent reinforcement of skills to continue to be engaged and motivated, while other learners need less frequent and consistent reinforcement. Different learners will have different levels of learning endurance.

4. Design Your Game

Start small or go big, and remember all great games always begin in beta and can always receive an update. There are no limits to the fun and creativity you can bring to your game.

Ask yourself the following questions to get started:

1. **Will students work alone or in teams?**
2. **How will players earn points?**
3. **How will you give out points?**
4. **What will students be able to do with their points?**

5. What will your game space look like?

6. How will you display the leaderboard or show game progress?

7. Will your game have tokens, power ups, badges, or other add-ons?

8. What will your marketplace be?

9. Will your game include mini-challenges or quests?

10. Will your game have bonuses?

5. Add Components to Help Students Reach Goals

Here are just a few components to consider adding to your game:

POWERS OR POWER CARDS
Special, valuable items or cards that players can earn or purchase. They give players extra abilities or powers. In a classroom, they can be anything that will engage and entice students, from using the teacher's chair to asking a classmate for help on a test question.

ITEMS
These may be bought to add to property or add to what the player can charge or earn.

LEVEL UP
Bonuses that can require multiple tasks or behaviors to achieve for a sizeable reward.

BADGES
Can add to the aesthetics of a the game board, multiply the points the player will earn, or be exchanged for a special privilege.

COUPONS, TICKETS, RANDOM BONUSES, OR DISCOVERIES
Can add surprise and new energy to the fun of the game.

MYSTERY LEVELS, QUESTS, BONUS LEVELS
Add extra challenging skill requirements, tasks, or learning projects for players to earn additional points, badges, or other resources.

MARKETPLACE
Players can buy, sell, swap, or trade with each other and with you.

MINI-GAMES

A short game contained within or added on to the existing game. It is always smaller or more simplistic than the larger game. Great to add at random times throughout the game to boost the objectives, engagement, or focus.

6. Design Your Score Board

Score boards share information about how each player is doing , demonstrating to students what their opponents have that they do not. Score boards can be as simple as notecards displayed on a bulletin board or as complex as digital tools like Schoology or Google Apps for Education tools. I use a bulletin board as my score board. Cardstock paper holds information about who each player is, how many stars they, earned, and the properties and other elements they have received. The scoreboard is just as valuable as the game, since it's the component of the game that keeps students wanting to play and reinforces your goals. When selecting the platform for your score board it is important to make sure you can easily maintain and update it regularly.

As I enter my third year of gamifying my classroom, my fifth game, and my second year-long game, my passion and belief in the power of gamification and its impact on education has never been stronger. Each day I can't wait to get to my classroom, to create or add new elements, and to imagine the next game. My students question, wonder out loud, and are hungry for what is next. I smile at their happiness and the mystery, curiosity, fun, anticipation, engagement, and excitement gamification has added to my classroom. It's immeasurable and something no amount of XP can buy!

SECTION 2

Homebrews & Game Sharks

Gamification Strategies & Tools to Utilize Across Content Areas

6

Scavenger Hunts

By RACHELLE DENE POTH

ISTE Standards for Students

5 Computational Thinker. Students develop and employ strategies for understanding and solving problems in ways that leverage the power of technological methods to develop and test solutions.

  b. Students collect data or identify relevant data sets, use digital tools to analyze them, and represent data in various ways to facilitate problem solving and decision making.

  c. Students break problems into component parts, extract key information, and develop descriptive models to understand complex systems or facilitate problem solving.

6 Creative Communicator. Students communicate clearly and express themselves creatively for a variety of purposes using the platforms, tools, styles, formats, and digital media appropriate to their goals.

  b. Students create original works or responsibly repurpose or remix digital resources for new creations.

  c. Students communicate complex ideas clearly and effectively by creating or using a variety of digital objects such as visualizations, models or simulations.

Whether technology-based or in a traditional paper format, creating a scavenger hunt is a great way to have students accomplish learning objectives. Scavenger hunts allow students to get up and move so they are, active rather than sitting and listening to a lecture. The main purpose of the hunt is to promote content-based skills and give students interesting and creative ways to practice those skills in a setting that expands beyond the traditional classroom.

Why Use Scavenger Hunts?

Scavenger hunts involve all students, help build a peer collaboration community, and strengthen relationships. Using a scavenger hunt is a means to accomplish many of the important tasks that teachers have, in a creative, fun, and engaging way.

How Does It Work?

All it takes to get started gamifying your classroom with a scavenger hunt is creating different tasks and assigning a point value to motivate students. I've found students take more risks or accept a greater challenge when earning points is the incentive. Here are some things to take into consideration while designing your scavenger hunt:

Partnerships or Teams

It's nice to have students pair up whether it be randomly or self-selected. Sometimes I find that randomly assigning groups helps make connections in the classroom, and it's a good way to make sure all students are included.

Time

You can give your students a set time within school hours or a deadline that carries over in an ongoing assignment. Similar to flipped or blended learning, in a scavenger hunt the work is engaging and students want to do it because it's different and unique.

The Tasks

What are the tasks students will accomplish? The nice thing about a scavenger hunt is that while the tasks or challenges are all the same, not all the same responses will be gathered by the students. Adapt the type of tasks you have and make them relevant to the material being covered in class.

Technology Versus Pen and Paper

Technology is great for further involving students, expanding learning, and providing limitless resources to help students achieve mastery and to continue their growth in various content areas. I created a scavenger hunt modeled after an app called *Goose Chase*. I came up with a list of tasks I wanted students to complete to reinforce the vocabulary they had studied throughout the year but also to let them to have some fun, especially at the end of the year when it seemed student engagement and motivation had been declining.

Example

Here is an example list from a scavenger hunt I used with my class. It is in Spanish, the English translation follows.

> Habla español con alguien en la clase de matemáticas o francés. Escribe tus nombres en una hoja de papel.

> Saca una foto de alguien nadando.

> Canta con el director de la escuela.

> Baila con tus amigos enfrente de un lugar donde hay libros y computadoras.

> Haz algo comico con tu grupo.

> Hay un incendio ¿Qué necesitas para apagarlo? Saca una foto.

> Busca a una persona que levanta pesas.

Translation:

> Speak Spanish with someone in math or French class. Write your names on a piece of paper.

> Take a picture of someone swimming.

> Sing with the principal of the school.

> Dance with your friends in front of a place where there are books and computers.

> Do something funny with your group.

> There is a fire. What do you need to put it out? Take a picture.

> Find someone who is lifting weights.

Resources

Appear In (**appear.in**) is a conferencing app that enables teachers to send directions or live video instructions to students as they move about the school to complete certain scavenger hunt tasks.

Goose Chase (**www.goosechase.com**) is an app that has preset tasks for a scavenger hunt, and enables the user to add tasks or use those from the list provided. The teacher can assign point values and a live feed is updated as students complete each task and post their proof.

7

The Amazing Race Challenge

By MICHELE HAIKEN

ISTE Standards for Students

2 Digital Citizen. Student recognize the rights, responsibilities and opportunities of living, learning and working in an interconnected digital world, and they act and model in ways that are safe, legal and ethical.

> b. Students engage in positive, safe, legal and ethical behavior when using technology, including social interactions online or when using networked devices.

3 Knowledge Constructor. Students critically curate a variety of resources using digital tools to construct knowledge, produce creative artifacts and make meaningful learning experiences for themselves and others.

> c. Student curate information from digital resources using a variety of tools and methods to create collections of artifacts that demonstrate meaningful connections or conclusions.

Turn lessons and classroom activities into a competitive, collaborative ac tivity that can take place beyond the walls of the classroom. Students work in teams or small groups to complete various content-specific tasks. Using game strategies and the format from the prime-time television game show *The Amazing Race,* students work in teams completing various tasks that unlock clues to the next task until they make it to the "finish line."

Why Use *The Amazing Race* Challenge?

In this challenge, students are working collaboratively to achieve a specific goal. The tasks are differentiated and allow students to move around during class time. Depending on the types of activities created, students are also working on skill building and critical thinking.

How Does It Work?

Determine your goals for what students will learn, understand, or be able to do after the lesson. Create three to six different activities you might use as learning stations or classroom activities. Create tasks that tap into multiple intelligences and Bloom's Taxonomy of Questions for the differentiated activities students will complete.

Think about places around school to plant clues where students will complete the various tasks. Map out a route and develop clues that will help students find next location. You might also post each clue as a QR code for students to uncover.

Post clues around the school and create a tracking sheet to help students record their responses. Start teams at staggered stations so they're not all starting from the same point.

After the teams have completed the *Amazing Race* Challenge, meet together to reflect and debrief what students gleaned from the activity. See what connections they made, which questions were answered, and which were left unanswered.

Example: *To Kill a Mockingbird Amazing Race* Challenge

While reading Harper Lee's *To Kill a Mockingbird*, students spent two class periods working in teams of four to five students to complete the *To Kill a Mockingbird* (TKAM) *Amazing Race* Challenge. Students followed clues from the text that led them around the school completing activities which in turn led other clues (see Figures 7.1a and 7.1b for examples of the challenge cards the students received). The first team who to complete all the tasks and discover all the clues won.

Clue 1

Scout said, "Until I feared I would lose it, I never loved to read." Where can Scout fuel her passion for reading? Here is where you can find the next task on your TKAM *Amazing Race*.

Task 1: A Nightmare Among Us, Chapter 15

Read the article *Fear Factor: How Herd Mentality Drives Us* (**goo.gl/g0p8KP**)

Answer three questions to make a tic-tac-toe win. Write your responses on the answer sheet provided and bring it to class completed.

Clue 2

In Chapter 11, Atticus told Jem that Mrs. Dubose was "old and ill." Where do you go when you feel ill? You should be able to get a clean bill of health while there and find your next clue.

Task 2: Gender Codes

In Chapters 11, 12, and 13 Scout is reminded by others to "act like a lady."

Read through the article *Growing Up Female in the 1930s South* (**goo.gl/c2RzhJ**). Think about what connections you can make between the women interviewed and the women in the book.

Complete the compare and contrast diagram in your Interactive English Notebook identifying similarities and differences between the gender expectations for women during this period and the gender expectations set upon Scout by Calpurnia and Aunt Alexandra.

Clue 3

DETOUR: Return to the classroom

Task 3: Caste Systems in Maycomb, Chapter 13

What is a caste system?

Caste systems, social inequalities, and poverty cycles are all important social themes in *To Kill a Mockingbird*. Throughout the book, there are divisions in social classes which cause tension and conflict.

What is the hierarchy in Maycomb County? Complete the chart on your answer sheet by placing where you think each of the characters belong. Then, find evidence from the text to support your claim.

Clue 4

We don't have a jail in school, but if you were to get in trouble you might be held up in this office. Stop by and say hello before you pick up your next clue.

Task 4: Different Dialects, Chapter 12

In Chapter 12, Scout and Jem attend church with Calpurnia. They notice that she uses language differently at church than she does in their home. Scout describes Calpurnia as "having command of two languages."

Use your text to examine the conversation between Jem, Scout, and Calpurnia at the end of Chapter 12. Respond to the following questions, using quotes from the book to help explain your responses.

A) How do Scout and Jem describe the way Calpurnia uses language in church?

B) What explanation does Calpurnia give for using language differently at church than in the Finch's home?

Clue 5

Sheriff Heck Tate oversees the safety and security of the townspeople in Maycomb Country. Who takes care of the safety and security of our school? He holds your next clue.

Task 5: Courage

At the end of Chapter 11 Atticus tells Jem, "I wanted you to see what real courage is, instead of getting the idea that courage is a man with a gun in his hand."

How do you define courage?

Who shows courage in the novel? Complete the chart on your answer sheet illustrating two characters who exemplify courage, how they show courage, and specific textual evidence that supports your claim.

Clue 6

During the 1930's most women cooked and prepared the food for their families as Calpurnia and Aunt Alexandra did for Jem, Scout, and Atticus. While you're in school, where can you get closest to a home-cooked meal? Find your next clue and maybe something sweet left over from Aunt Alexandra's tea party.

Task 6: Life Lessons

Find three people (young people or adults) who can tell you the important life lessons they remember from reading *To Kill a Mockingbird*.

Use your phone or a borrowed device to video record this person talking about their memories of the book and the important life lessons they took away from the it.

Clue Answers

1. **The Library**

2. **Nurse's Office**

3. **Classroom**

4. **Principal's Office**

5. **Security Office**

6. **Cafeteria**

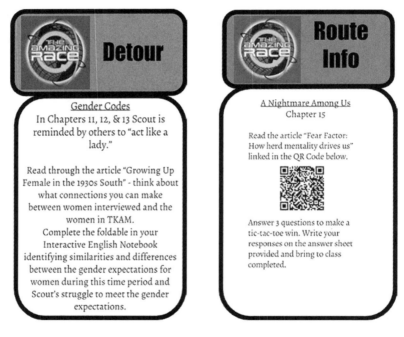

Figures 7.1a and 7.1b. Challenge cards for TKAM Amazing Race.

8

Classcraft

By TRAVIS PHELPS

ISTE Standards for Students

2 Digital Citizen. Students recognize the rights, responsibilities and opportunities of living, learning and working in an interconnected digital world, and they act and model in ways that are safe, legal and ethical.

5 Computational Thinker. Students develop and employ strategies for understanding and solving problems in ways that leverage the power of technological methods to develop and test solutions.

7 Global Collaborator. Students use digital tools to broaden their perspectives and enrich their learning by collaborating with others and working effectively in teams locally and globally.

Classcraft is a role-playing game platform where students have unique avatars and class roles that dictate their actions. Students earn or lose points based on their actions. Gamification allows teachers and students to have fun in the learning process, and using *Classcraft* can help develop a positive class climate where students get excited about a game that's tied to their learning and responsibilities.

Why Use *Classcraft*?

Classcraft can engage students who are difficult to motivate and increase engagement for all students, not just those who typically excel. It's especially valuable for secondary students who don't yet have clear self-direction, but need more motivation than primary students.

Implementing *Classcraft* also builds relationships, adds a climate of fun and spontaneity to the classroom, and creates memories and habits that foster community and culture. Some students will always remember learning with *Classcraft*.

How Does *Classcraft* Work?

Classcraft has four types of points: experience points (XP), health points (HP), action points (AP), and gold points (GP). Teachers typically reward students with XP and issue consequences by taking away HP. Students use AP for specified actions in the class and typically gain GP by training their pets (though teachers can also reward students with GP).

Students are divided into three different types of characters: warriors, healers, and mages. Warriors have a high amount of HP, so they can take damage for a team. Healers can heal players who have been harmed by using their AP. Mages can perform special actions by using their AP, which are typically fun for the team.

Students gain XP by completing tasks assigned by the teacher or gamemaster. These tasks might include meeting learning objectives, completing class jobs, participating in group work, or behaving appropriately. As students gain more XP, they level up for every 1,000 XP earned. Whenever they level up, they earn what is called a power. A power is an activity that students initiate by spending AP. These powers might include taking HP damage from another group member, healing another player, or—depending on how a teacher sets up the game—could include asking the teacher to sing a song in front of the class or making the teacher provide a baked good for the player's group. If a player loses all his or her HP, he or she "falls in battle." A random consequence selector chooses a consequence, which can include cleaning part of the classroom, writing a paragraph on the student's behavior, or if the student is lucky, no consequence.

While it's challenging for teachers new to gamification to wrap their brains around these various types of points and what they entail, students catch on very quickly, and the game becomes a highly motivating learning adventure.

Example

Classcraft is beneficial for me as an eigth grade teacher organizing and maintaining a classroom with tasks like gathering paperwork for the office, collecting permission slips, handing out any office forms, writing down homework assignments on the homework board, and cleaning up at the end of the day. Students earn XP for completing these or lose HP for neglecting their duties.

Getting middle schoolers excited about grammar can be daunting, to say the least. I thus implemented a system to turn grammar into a game. I would present a grammar exercise to the class, and then give students a set amount of time to complete it individually (usually one to two minutes), followed by time to work collaboratively (also usually one to two minutes). I would then take advantage of *Classcraft*'s "Wheel of Destiny," which randomly selects a student to perform the grammar exercise at the board. If the student get the answer correct, the student and their small group gains XP, and if not, the entire group will lose HP.

Resources

Classcraft: **http://classcraft.com**

INTERVIEW

Shawn Young, Classcraft *CEO and Co-Founder*

Michele Haiken: What does gamification mean to you?

Shawn Young: Gamification has become a bit of an umbrella term in the last few years—people apply the term to anything where you can gain points or badges. Not surprisingly, seeing gamification from this lens leads to experiences which can feel stale, boring or lack meaning.

For me, gamification is much more than that. In fact, I prefer the term *ludicization, which means:* "To create a situation from which play can emerge." In this sense, gamification becomes the art of crafting experiences in which many of the components of games (autonomy, competency, social relationships, randomness, feedback, etc.) can be applied to create a state of playfulness. Using these components leads to genuine fun (with a purpose) from which intrinsic motivations can stem. Simply put, good gamification is applying extrinsic motivators that will be internalized to produce intrinsic motivation.

MH: As a former teacher, what do you see as the benefits of gamification for teachers and students?

SY: This depends on the approach, really. With *Classcraft*, we help teachers gamify the *experience* of coming to school, rather than gamifying content, like you would see with math or language games. From that perspective, the benefits to classroom culture are huge: students are taking ownership of the way the classroom is run and are significantly more engaged, even with the rote day-to-day tasks that occur naturally in class life. The game is very collaborative, so students have a team that's looking out for them, and they face challenges together. They also get much more positive reinforcement than they're used to, which has a big impact on their perception of self-worth. Obviously, this is great for teachers, who feel like they're working with students, not against them.

MH: How did you first get involved in gaming for education? When and how did *Classcraft* come to fruition?

SY: *Classcraft* stemmed out of my own unique background as a grade 11 physics teacher, web developer and gamer. I have been playing board games and video games since I was a kid and that continued into my adult life. As an educator, I related culturally with my students—indeed, we were playing the same games! I had a poor school experience growing up, often feeling like I was wasting my time, so my main focus as a teacher was to ensure coming to school was pertinent for students, and that they felt it was too.

It dawned on me that the experience of coming to school would be much more satisfying if it was like an RPG, so I made a quick prototype and started playing with my students. I fine-tuned the game over the course of three years before making a little website to share with other teachers what I was doing. Overnight, the website attracted 150,000 visits—it seemed a lot of other people were interested in gamifying their classrooms! I then teamed up with my brother, Devin, who is a designer, and our father Lauren, who has 35 years of experience in business and accounting, and *Classcraft* was born. Since then, the platform has evolved tremendously.

MH: What are some of the elements from classic video games that can benefit teachers and students for gamification purposes?

SY: When thinking of this question, people tend to look for tropes—"Should I use XP and levels?", "Do students need an avatar?" and "Should I lay this out on a map?" are typical questions that come up. At Classcraft, our focus is more on the fundamental psychology of self -determination theory and how it applies to video games. There is a reason gamers are willing to spend hours repeating the same boring task to complete an objective, but aren't willing to spend five minutes doing math homework: games fulfill seven fundamental motivational needs (autonomy, competency, relationships, discovery, surprise, feedback, storytelling). These are the elements we lifted from games to design a playful experience, and they are outlined on our blog (**classcraft.com/blog**).

MH: What life skills and Common Core State Standards do *Classcraft* and gamification address?

SY: *Classcraft* is very customizable: it can be used to develop any soft skills by identifying behaviors that show mastery and awarding points for that. For example, if you want to develop grit in your students, you'll identify behaviors that are indicative of grit, like persevering in the face of adversity, and give students points for those behaviors, thus encouraging explicitly to internalize them. Because these behaviors are logged in the game, you'll be able to assess development of these skills by looking at the per-student behavior analytics in the platform. That being said, *Classcraft* explicitly fosters meaningful teamwork, ownership of learning, prosocial skills and perseverance. In terms of CCSS, *Classcraft* doesn't gamify curriculum, it gamifies the experience.

MH: You have said that "when playing video games, kids feel a sense of empowerment." Can you talk more about that?

SY: In a video game, the player inherently knows that they can succeed. Even in the face of the most difficult challenges, they can try as often as they'd like to develop their skills. Often kids can tackle problems in several ways and make meaningful choices about their trajectory within the game. All of this leads to a sense that the player can shape their destiny and build mastery for success.

Compare this to the school experience: kids often have only one set way to complete their journey through a course, and they only get one chance to demonstrate mastery of a given piece of content. That doesn't feel very empowering.

MH: As the gamemaster for *Classcraft*, what are you dreaming up and working on now for teachers to benefit from your gaming platform?

SY: We've got a lot of things coming! One thing we're focused on is integrating with more platforms and partners. We're already integrated with Google Classroom and Microsoft's Office 365, and we want to create more opportunities for teachers to be able to gamify the entire student experience, no matter which platforms and tools they're using. We are also looking at building more game features, like self-correcting quizzes students can complete for XP and storylines they can play throughout the year.

MH: What has been the best thing about creating *Classcraft* and sharing it with teachers all around the world?

SY: This may sound hokey, but it's been really great for everyone on the team to see the profoundly positive impact we have had on teachers, students, and parents. Every day, we receive videos, pictures, and testimonials from people using *Classcraft* telling us how it has changed their lives for the better. From the shy fifth-grader who wrote us to tell she had finally been able to make friends because of *Classcraft*, to the burned-out teacher who has found the love of teaching again, to the parent who is raving about how motivated their child is, all of these testimonials act as fuel to keep us imagining new ways to make the classroom a better place.

MH: Since gaming and gamification is continuously evolving, where do you see it going? What do you see as the future of gamification for educational purposes in the next year, five years, and even ten years from now?

SY: Who knows! It's an exciting time in the field. Tech is changing faster than we can anticipate and opportunities like virtual and augmented reality will have an impact. I'm certain we'll see gamification become much more prevalent, as educators see success stories and jump on board.

9

Sydney's World

By IVAN KALTMAN

ISTE Standards for Students

1 Empowered Learner. Students leverage technology to take an active role in choosing, achieving and demonstrating competency in their learning goals, informed by the learning sciences.

> c. Students use technology to seek feedback that informs and improves their practice and to demonstrate their learning in a variety of ways.

6 Creative Communicator. Students communicate clearly and express themselves creatively for a variety of purposes using the platforms, tools, styles, formats, and digital media appropriate to their goals.

Sydney's World is a full middle grade fiction novel of text housed within an RPG (role-playing game) video game. Students read the fictional story through character dialogue, the perfect format for turn-taking read alouds. Reading passages are broken up with exploration, puzzles, and occasional battles, which provide immersion, enabling attention and focus to be sustained.

According to the game's website, *Sydney's World* focuses on the intersecting story arcs of a young girl searching for her father and a king in search of redemption. Sydney is a realistic eight-year-old girl, behaving just as any eight-year old would; alternating between cuteness, petulance, innocence, anger, sorrow, illogical decisions, jealousy, and great joy (SydneysWorld1, 2013).

When she is captured by an evil wizard and transported to another world, Sydney's toy elf, Snowball, is brought to life. He is Sydney's alter ego and his whole existence revolves around her. Together, they stop small dogs from barking, cause a king to reconsider his philosophy, and deal with very real emotions in a fantasy world setting.

Why Use *Sydney's World*?

The game design of Sydney's has been vetted by the world's largest gaming community (the game is commercially distributed by Steam at **store.steampowered.com**) and has been reviewed and recommended by educators as well as the gaming community.

Sydney's World encourages close reading. As a quest-based game, students must read, recall, and understand information in order to know what to do and where to go next.

The visual format has advantages over traditional text, since there is much less text per screen than a book page, so words are much easier to visually perceive and track.

Sydney's World supports English Language Arts Common Core State Standards. Preparation for Learning (PFL) assessments, teacher's guides (including essential questions and teacher-led reflection), and curriculum-based activities and projects are in development.

How Does It Work?

In *Sydney's World*, the text itself is differentiated. All students are challenged (without being overwhelmed) by reading character text on the edge of their regime of competence. Text is read aloud in small groups (using mini-laptops), divided into teams. Each team is comprised of readers at different levels.

All text in *Sydney's World* is multimodal, so all students get a solid grasp of the literature essentials (characters, setting, plot, themes, etc.), as opposed to textbooks, worksheets, and novels, which don't appeal to a variety of learning types. Multimodal text allows all students to engage in further curriculum-based language arts instruction with greater understanding and interest.

The story text is always accompanied by illustrations, including the characters who are talking, similar to a graphic novel. Hundreds of sentences are ready by professional voice actors along with text to enhance understanding and immersion without boring narration (which is the chief complaint of students using audiobooks).

Sydney's World encourages inclusion. All students in a class (including students in special education and English language learners) can play together, regardless of reading ability.

Typical scenarios that bring anxiety to weaker readers (being called on to read at random intervals, fearing the text will be too difficult, anticipating they may lose their place) are all mitigated by the way text is presented. There are additional roles besides reader including explorer, battler, navigator, problem-solver), which allow students to be valued for intellectual abilities other than reading.

The game design prohibits any student from going ahead, making stronger readers "reading buddies" who follow the text at the same pace and help less strong readers.

Sydney's World expands the vocabulary of all students. Research by James Gee shows that children develop vocabulary through meaningful dialogue with adults and advanced peers (2008). *Sydney's World* incorporates this strategy twofold: the characters themselves fulfill the role of conveying meaningful dialogue with adults, and the game is designed to be played with advanced peers and teachers reading the more difficult character text and providing definitions and examples if needed.

According to the game website, *"Sydney's World* has a robust vocabulary of 570 words above grade-level spread throughout the game in 32 distinct areas" (SydneysWorld1, 2013). All vocabulary from the game has situated meaning (images, embodied actions, emotions, and experiences) from a virtual world that every student can relate to regardless of reading level. Vocabulary is significantly more likely to be learned naturally through gameplay, peer collaboration, and teacher guidance than traditional worksheets or textbooks where words are memorized to match with other words for tests.

References

SydneysWorld1. (2013). [Game website] Retrieved from **http://www.sydney-sworld1.com**

10

World War I Trench Simulation with *Minecraft*

By ROBERT M. DALY

5 Computational Thinker. Students develop and employ strategies for understanding and solving problems in ways that leverage the power of technological methods to develop and test solutions.

   b. Students collect data or identify relevant data sets, using digital tools to analyze them, and represent data in various ways to facilitate problem solving and decision making.

   c. Students break problems into component parts, extract key information, and develop descriptive models to understand complex systems or facilitate problem solving.

6 Creative Communicator. Students communicate clearly and express themselves creatively for a variety of purposes using the platforms, tools, styles, formats, and digital media appropriate to their goals.

   b. Students create original works or responsibly repurpose or remix digital resources for new creations.

   c. Students communicate complex ideas clearly and effectively by creating or using a variety of digital objects such as visualizations, models or simulations.

Minecraft, and its educational counterpart *MinecraftEdu*, is a game where the player spawns into a virtual world with the task of manipulating the landscape in order to progress and survive. The creative mode of the game provides even more customizable options with endless possibilities for collaboration among players.

Minecraft requires players to dig into the ground in search of raw materials. Within a few minutes observing *Minecraft* for the first time, I immediately realized I had found the perfect platform for a realistic World War I (WWI) trench warfare simulation.

After reading Erich Maria Remarque's *All Quiet on the Western Front*, studying WWI, and researching trench diagrams, students work together on two separate teams (as adversarial nations). Students can design, create, and defend their own trench fortification lines in a virtual landscape tailor-made specifically for this project. After several sessions of planning and creation, student teams are given the opportunity to engage in combat against each other. This simulation provides opportunities for students to experience the burdens, horrors, and emotions of being a soldier in the trenches during WWI, without any true physical or emotional threat.

Students become completely immersed in the world of the simulation and enjoy applying their knowledge of WWI and trench warfare as they develop strategies, execute their designs, and attack enemy trenches. After experiencing the simulation, students are excited to share the strong connections they make between their actions and emotions during game play, the characters of *All Quiet on the Western Front*, and actual life WWI histories and testimonials.

Why Use *Minecraft*?

To help my students understand difficult and introspective concepts surrounding war, like the physical horrors of warfare, lack of humanity, loss of identity, and brotherhood in arms, I chose to present a video game simulation alongside the material covered in class.

The *Minecraft* WWI trench warfare simulation provides students with a safe, engaging, and interactive way to experience warfare. All students are interacting at the same time in one collaborative world. The *MinecraftEdu* version of the software allows for the teacher to create custom worlds, pause gameplay, and turn on and off a player versus player mode so students can experience the emotions and consequences of combat.

When prompted to reflect on the simulation, students see how easily they could lose themselves to violence, fear, or vengeance. Students can understand the feelings, motivations, and decisions made by characters in the book and by those who fought on the battlefields.

Students experience building trenches, having downtime, witnessing the catastrophic effect on the landscape, and observing the consequence and carnage of combat. These collective experiences provide students with several avenues to connect to, understand, and analyze the themes from *All Quiet on the Western Front* and the actual experiences in World War I.

The video game setting allows for natural excitement, collaboration, and most importantly, provides an opportunity for a student to excel and achieve in a non-traditional classroom setting. Students who may not speak up often in class, lack confidence, or struggle with their writing skills may shine during game play. Several students play games of some variety, and a video game simulation provides an opportunity for students to demonstrate knowledge and think critically while using "tools" they may be more comfortable with, and use on an everyday basis in their personal lives.

How Does It Work?

The beauty of using *Minecraft* is the flexibility it allows the teacher. You can make your virtual world and student tasks as complex or as simple as you wish. You can consider your own game skills, the time you can devote to creating and playing the simulation, and the specific tasks for students to focus on. *MinecraftEdu* provides the educator with several vital tools that allow you to create a custom-made world, including what you want and need to make your specific simulation successful.

The fundamental element of *Minecraft* involves digging, thus creating trenches is basic gameplay accessible even to a novice. A simple exercise where students spawn into the world, get into assigned groups, spread out, and create their own trench lines would not require much prior knowledge of the game, and a stand alone "trench building activity" could be conducted in one class period.

For a more intense multi-day simulation of trench building and combat, students are divided into two teams, and each is assigned a side of the battle field to build their fortifications. Students are asked to work together to build a trench line that mirrors the maps and diagrams they have studied. After adequate planning and construction time is allotted, the teacher turns on the PvP mode, allowing for combat. In this mode, students' avatars have health bars and need to avoid losing health points, or face a virtual death. They also must avoid enemy fire (in the form of bow and arrow or blunt weapon attack), drowning, falls, and other hazards.

Depending on the desired learning objectives, combat can be managed by the teacher in a variety of ways. One option is to create a "capture the flag" style of gameplay, where one group attacks and the other defends an object kept behind their trench lines. Another possibility is a total war style of gameplay where the student teams are simply tasked with the total annihilation of their enemies' ability to fight.

When combat occurs, students' gameplay resembles warfare as players run through the high grass, dive into shell holes to avoid explosives, and shoot down the enemy players as they approach their trench line. Players take damage, search for a place to hide, recover strength, and navigate through "no man's land" to attack an enemy trench—all while the simulation provides students a hands-on experience to combine with other traditional classroom experiences.

Student reflection is vital to learning in this process. During gameplay, students are constantly making connections between the history they have studied, their own feelings during the simulation, and the characters' feelings from *All Quiet on the Western Front*. Players with little experience consider themselves new recruits and look to veterans (those who play *Minecraft* regularly) for help and protection, mirroring the portrayal of new recruits in the novel. As students become engaged in survival, combat, and victory in the simulation, they are constantly making connections that help them understand and think about the fears, horrors, and loss of their humanity during warfare.

Students are asked to write a reflection each night as well as a culminating reflection at the end of the simulation that discusses the connections made, and understandings fostered during the experience.

Ensuring Success

Take the following into consideration when you're planning a simulation or activity using *Minecraft*.

> **Fair Teams:** Try and match up experienced players with novice players to make for an evenly matched simulation—a gameplay survey can help you discern each student's skill level.

> **World Building:** There are already several world templates shared and available online for use. You don't need to start from scratch if you don't have the time or ability. There are hundreds of worlds for you to explore and download.

> **Student Helpers:** You will be shocked by what your students can do. Let them know you are thinking of using *Minecraft* in the classroom and ask them if they have ideas or can help design the world template. Every year I have conducted the simulation, eager students are begging me to help tweak and upgrade the simulation to make the experience even better.

Unlimited Possibilities for Learning

Minecraft can be used for much more than war simulations. I found trench warfare was a natural fit due to *Minecraft*'s basic requirement to dig and build. Yet *Minecraft* could easily be used for a variety of historically themed simulations such as colonialism, the frontier, ancient civilizations, monument building, city planning, or recreations. Further, *Minecraft* has an open-ended number of possibilities for any subject, curriculum, or collaborative activity. I have seen *Minecraft* used to teach topics ranging from basic communication and collaboration skills to detailed projects that ask students to create a functioning animal cell using the materials in the game. The beauty of this platform is in its customizability.

Example: Trench Design

Simple trench design and construction offers students a way to demonstrate their content knowledge while working collaboratively with their classmates to meet specific tasks and challenges (see Figure 10.1).

Figure 10.1. Screenshot of *Minecraft* WWI trench scene.

A full combat simulation may require advanced planning and world forming on the part of the teacher (but it doesn't have to). Combat allows students to not only apply their knowledge of WWI by building trenches (see Figure 10.2), but provides an avenue to experience difficult concepts like; the significance of communication and planning, the value of food and supplies, and the impact of desensitization to violence.

Figure 10.2. Screenshot of *Minecraft* WWI scenes.

Example: Battlefield Fly Over or Walk Through

By providing students with a before and after view of the battlefield, students can develop an empathy and understanding of how rapid and drastic the disturbance of the landscape was during war. The several modes of *Minecraft* allow for many different perspectives. After battle, a battle field flyover allows students to see the destruction of the natural landscape, and provides them with a memorable visual. This works especially well as a retrospective activity. Students who find themselves enjoying "playing war" and "enemy kill counts" will have a chance to see

Figure 10.3 *Minecraft* WWI screenshot of aerial view of war damage and casualties.

the collateral damage caused (see Figure 10.3). This has the most impact when juxtaposed with an outdoor nature walk, and a chance for students to imagine a blissful forest becoming a moonlike wasteland.

Resources

Minecraft Educational Resources: **education.minecraft.net/minecraftedu/**

MinecraftEdu Wiki: **services.minecraftedu.com/wiki/Main_Page**

Teaching with *Minecraft*: **services.minecraftedu.com/wiki/ Teaching_with_MinecraftEdu**

Minecraft World Library: **services.minecraftedu.com/worlds/**

Wonderful World of Humanities: **services.minecraftedu.com/wiki/Wonderful_World_of_Humanities**

11

Adventure Quests

By MICHELE HAIKEN

ISTE Standards for Students

1 Empowered Learner. Students leverage technology to take an active role in choosing, achieving and demonstrating competency in their learning goals, informed by the learning sciences.

2 Digital Citizen. Students recognize the rights, responsibilities and opportunities of living, learning, and working in an interconnected digital world, and they act and model in ways that are safe, legal and ethical.

3 Knowledge Constructor. Students critically curate a variety of resources using digital tools to construct knowledge, produce creative artifacts and make meaningful learning experiences for themselves and others.

Quests are missions, tasks, events, and adventures with an objective. A quest is a long and arduous search for something. Quests require students to work independently or collaboratively to complete various missions or tasks. The teacher determines the parameters of the quest for students to complete.

Why Use Quests?

Quests can be self-directed exploration or a mission mapped out by the teacher. Adventure quests are fun side activities for motivating students to learn about a specific topic. Adventure quests can be adapted to any content area. During a quest, students are in charge of their own learning and it helps them engage with content material in a new way.

How Do Quests Work?

There are multiple ways to organize a quest. I offer various side quests for students to participate in for additional experience points (XP) each quarter or unit of study. The side quests related to what students are studying in class, or they can be individually driven to include an independent investigation conducted by the student.

Example: Investigative Journalism

The adventure quest described below was a 10-week trivia game I designed based on current events addressed in the news each week during an investigative journalism inquiry unit (see Figure 11.1).

With the use of Actively Learn (**activelylearn.com**), an online reading platform, Twitter, and Google Forms, I created a series of trivia-type questions. Each week one question was posted on my teacher website based on the article of the week. Students submitted their answers on a Google Form (see Figure 11.2). Each question was worth 50 XP. Additional gold points (GP) could be earned by going onto Twitter and searching the hashtag **#RMS8RQuest** to find more adventure quest

Fig. 11.1. Investigative Journalism Adventure Quest rules.

questions. The student with the most points at the end of the adventure quest earned an additional 1,500 XP *Classcraft* points *plus* a treasure (a $10 gift card).

Each question had a unique code that students had to input as well as their answer on the Google Form.

INVESTIGATIVE JOURNALISM ADVENTURE QUEST

QUESTION 6

Code – Run

Question – The Barkley Marathon takes place in which state?

CLICK HERE TO SUBMIT YOUR ANSWER . . .GOOD LUCK!

#RMS8RQuest

Figure 11.2. Sample question for adventure quest.

The Twitter questions were not based on the weekly readings, but on events happening in the news that specific day, so they were worth fewer points. Twitter questions included, "Who did President Obama nominate for the Supreme Court?" and "What Lego minifigure was unveiled this week?"

Resources

Actively Learn (**activelylearn.com**) is a digital reading platform that contains books, articles, poems, and speeches. Students join a "classroom" created by their teacher to read assigned digital texts and complete assignments within the workspace. Actively Learn offers teacher-designed assignments with ready-made questions. Teachers can also design their own questions and prompts.

Twitter: **twitter.com**

Google Forms: **gsuite.google.com/forms**

12

Grudgeball

By KRISTIE ORLANDO-BANGALI

ISTE Standards for Students

1 Empowered Learner. Students leverage technology to take an active role in choosing, achieving and demonstrating competency in their learning goals, informed by the learning sciences.

5 Computational Thinker. Students develop and employ strategies for understanding and solving problems in ways that leverage the power of technological methods to develop and test solutions.

*G*rudgeball is a review game where various teams battle to gain control of the grudgeboard to preserve their own pieces while taking away pieces from opponents. The objective is to be the team that has the most remaining pieces, or Xs, at the end of the game.

Why Use *Grudgeball*?

This high intensity game is a big motivator for students when used as a review game at the end of any unit of study. It can be modified across all grade levels and content areas. I first discovered this game on Pinterest, and I have since adapted it for use in my middle school Spanish classroom. My students often beg me to play this game! To play you need a small Nerf basketball hoop and ball. I prefer to create the grudgeboard (see Figure 12.1) using a Smart Notebook and display it on a Smart Board, however, setting up the board on a traditional whiteboard or poster board works just as well.

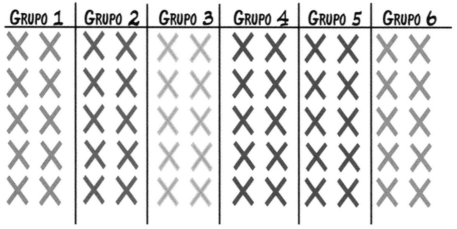

Figure 12.1. Sample grudgeboard created for Smart Board.

How Does *Grudgeball* Work?

Grudgeball is played in teams, with ideally four to five students per team. Each team plays against the other teams—usually there are six teams in total. The premise is that students answer various questions to gain the opportunity to take away Xs from their opponents—therein starting the grudges between teams. You will be quick to observe how students begin to form alliances with one another.

Here are the rules for students to follow:

Each Team Gets a Question

Any question and level of difficulty works! The team must answer as a team—all members must agree upon the answer that's given. Each team starts with 10 Xs. If a team gives the correct answer to a question, they automatically get to take away two Xs from the grudgeboard. They can take both from one team or split up the Xs to take away one X from two different teams. The team can't take Xs from themselves!

If they answer the question incorrectly, the following team has a chance to steal the question.

MODIFICATION

I like to have all teams write down the answer to every question to ensure that all teams are participating and paying attention throughout the game. This makes them accountable for reviewing all questions that are asked.

Shoot the Nerf Ball

Before they take away any Xs, the team is given a chance to increase their ability to gain more Xs. To do this, one player from the team is selected to shoot the Nerf ball.

Prior to the start of the game I set up a shooting line for a two-point shot and a three-point shot with tape on the floor. Teams can choose to shoot from the two- or three-point line.

A shoot and score from the two-point line will give the team two *extra* Xs to take away, making their total for that round four Xs!

A shoot and score from the three point line will give the team three *extra* Xs to take away, making their total for that round five Xs!

But, if the shooter misses the hoop, they only get to take away one X as opposed to the original two that they would have been afforded.

Elimination

If a team gets eliminated, which will invariably happen, they're not entirely out of the game. If a team is knocked off they will still be given a question to answer when it is their turn. However, to get back on the board the team *must* answer the question correctly *and* make a basket. If they do both, they can earn two or three Xs back on the grudgeboard depending on if they shoot from the two- or three-point line.

Winning the Game

I typically play for between 20 and 30 minutes during a typical 40-minute class. At the end of the game, the team with the most Xs remaining wins!

Boss Battles

By MICHELE HAIKEN

5 Computational Thinker. Students develop and employ strategies for understanding and solving problems in ways that leverage the power of technological methods to develop and test solutions.

    c. Students break problems into component parts, extract key information, and develop descriptive models to understand complex systems or facilitate problem solving.

6 Creative Communicator. Students communicate clearly and express themselves creatively for a variety of purposes using the platforms, tools, styles, formats, and digital media appropriate to their goals.

A "boss" in gaming is a villain who the hero must face and defeat to save the day. Think of the monster at the end of each level in the original *Super Marios Bros.* These characters must be defeated before moving to the next level. In classroom boss battles, students are working in teams or individually to beat the clock and answer questions, taking on the role of the hero and earning rewards for defeating the boss.

Why Use Boss Battles?

Boss battles can be used to review or test what students know and understand. Students have support of their team members in answering questions and can have an opportunity to try again if their first answer is incorrect. Boss battles transfer the pressure of a traditional test into engagement and excitement.

How Do Boss Battles Work?

The gamemaster (teacher) must select a boss for the students to battle. This boss can be a unique fictional character created specifically for the boss battle, or it can be a character from a game, movie, or book (see Figures 13.1 and 13.2).

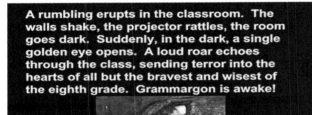

Figure 13.1. Screenshot introducing boss battle (Kessen, 2015).

The gamemaster creates the questions necessary for the boss battle to test the students, and decides the value of the boss and the value of each question. For every question the students answer correctly, they weaken the boss, but for every question that's answered incorrectly, the students lose health points or experience points.

The day of the boss battle, everyone has their own individual answer sheets. When a question is posted or read aloud, students have 30 seconds to read the question and answer it on their answer sheet. Once an answer is written down, it cannot be erased or changed.

The boss selects or "attacks" a random student. If the student answers the question correctly, the boss is dealt damage but if the question is answered incorrectly, the boss will "attack" the student and diminish his or her game points.

The student can dodge the damage if a teammate has the correct answer. If a teammate supplies an incorrect answer, then the the entire team will take the damage.

Figure 13.2. boss battle challenge (Kessen, 2015).

Example: Grammargon

Mallory Kessen, a seventh-grade language arts teacher at Walnut Hills High School in Cincinnati, OH, uses boss battles in her class for final reviews and assessments. Figures 13.1 and 13.2 are from a battle she used as an end of semester review against Grammargon. For more details about how she uses and designs her boss battles, visit her education blog at **mallorykessen.weebly.com/education-blog**.

SECTION 3

Cheats

Gamification Strategies for Success

14

Head of the Class

> Designing Effective Leaderboards for Gamified Learning Environments

By CHRIS HESSELBEIN

It was a good race. I had my fair share of wipeouts but I fought hard to reclaim the lead. There was only one more thing to do: enter my initials so that all others who attempted this feat could gaze upon my glory. I turned the wheel to navigate to my first initial, C, and hit the gas pedal to select it. I spun the wheel again and the letters frantically scrolled by. The clock was ticking. I overshot R, wasting precious seconds. I corrected and hit the pedal again. I cranked the wheel left toward H as the clock ran out. The initials were entered: CRJ. So close. The year was 1986. The game was *Pole Position*, a Formula One style racing game. My high score, 234th place, lasted for about a week until they unplugged the game to vacuum the floor of the local pizza place.

What Are Leaderboards?

Pole Position, like many arcade games, has a leaderboard: a ranked list of players' top scores. The leaderboard itself isn't the primary reason why people are drawn to play arcade games. It's most likely that people play *Pole Position* because it gives them a chance to drive a racecar at mind blurring speeds while operating a clutchless two-speed manual transmission, a rarity in modern day video motorsports. Leaderboards don't excel at motivating initial player buy in. However, they do play a part in motivating players to drop even more quarters into the slot and play again (Burgers, Eden, et al., 2015). They encourage continued participation as players compete against their own previous best scores along with the scores of others. It's for this reason that leaderboards are a valuable feature of the gamified classroom.

Gamified systems need a feedback mechanism—a way to let players see progress. Leaderboards can provide feedback on progress in two ways: cumulatively and relatively. They can give updates on cumulative individual progress by showing the total number of points accrued over a given time and display this progress relative to others on the leaderboard. When players see evidence of growth they are intrinsically motivated to continue by an improved sense of competency (Ryan & Deci, 2000). When players see the growth of others, they may feel motivated to adjust their own behaviors to keep pace with the group. For example, if I step on a scale and see that I have lost two pounds, I feel that my workout routine is paying off and I feel energized to do it more often. If I find out that my exercise group on average has lost three pounds I might feel like I have to step up my game to keep up with my friends. Both cumulative and relative feedback, when displayed on a leaderboard, can help players push themselves to the limits of their performance potential through personal goals and friendly competition.

The ranked nature of the progress display gives the leaderboard a sense of directionality. There is only one way players want to move on the leaderboard: up. A player can tell when they pass another player, or when they get passed, in their push toward the coveted number one spot. That rank comes with status. Players will fight for that status, both to keep it and usurp it. The goal of using a leaderboard in a gamified classroom is to leverage the allure of that public status to motivate all players to strive to do their best. When it comes to competitive feedback, leaderboards are in first place.

However, for every student who claws their way up a position, there is another student who gets pushed down. If the intent of using a leaderboard is to motivate all students to move toward the top, by design, a leaderboard fails in this endeavor. In order for there to be winners, there must also be losers. Dr. Seuss captures this dynamic very well in *Yertle the Turtle* (Geisel, 1950), as a turtle named Mack exclaims,

> *Your Majesty, please... I don't like to complain,*
> *But down here below, we are feeling great pain.*
> *I know, up on top you are seeing great sights,*
> *But down here at the bottom we, too, should have rights.*

For every student who takes pride in their growth, there will be another student feeling negatively about losing their ranking. Some suggest that this aversion to being lower in the stack could motivate students to aspire to achieve more. However, more often than not, I find that this constant state of losing demoralizes the lower half of the leaderboard, risking disengagement from the activity, and, therefore, from the learning (Nicholson, 2013).

Fame and Shame

Leaderboards operate on two motivators: fame and shame. They work on the assumption that all students will want to be on top, or at least not on the bottom; simultaneously activating both positive and negative feedback systems (Kluger & DeNisi, 1996). The promise of fame is motivating for those who have it within their reach. However, is this type of drive worth activating the other side of the motivational coin, shame? No matter how hard they try, some students will regularly be on the bottom of the leaderboard. If this condition persists, students may perceive their situation as out of their control, creating a self-fulfilling spiral of learned helplessness where students give up before they even begin (Abramson, Seligman, & Teasdale, 1978). These students will probably be the ones already struggling to accomplish even the smallest tasks. Should a teacher ever attempt to use shame to motivate their students? I think not. Shaming techniques might evoke small, immediate behavior modifications but will not promote long term student growth. Luckily, there are ways to reduce the amount of shame inherent in leaderboards.

Anonymity

An easy way to take some shame out of a leaderboard is by managing the identities displayed on the board itself. A teacher can do this by using avatars: alternative identities derived from the game world. In lieu of using a student's real name on a leaderboard, use a nickname, a codename, a number, or the name of a character in the game. Not using the real name of the student puts a little psychological distance between the student and the leaderboard rank. This isn't a perfect solution since eventually, in a tightly-knit learning environment, players will begin to figure out the real identities of the avatars on the leaderboard. However, this method can take the sting out of the leaderboard ranking by giving at least a sense of anonymity to the player.

Scope

Another way to make a leaderboard less uncomfortable is to adjust the scope of the leaderboard. Instead of displaying a whole class, consider only displaying some of the rankings. Better yet, only make certain rankings visible to certain people. A popular version of this is only displaying the top 10 or 20 ranked players. This method makes sure that the lower ranked players don't feel bad about being displayed at the bottom of the list. But if players are not displayed, how do they get the feedback needed on their progress? This is when it would be nice to get a personalized leaderboard report. Imagine a student periodically receiving their rank privately with only the two players directly above and below them in the rankings. This would show each player what they would have to do to catch the next players and stay away from the ones behind them. In essence, giving private motivation without public shaming (see Table 14.1).

PROGRESS UPDATE	AVATAR NAME	LEVEL	POINT GAP
Catching up to	Gandalf	13	+76
You	Frodo	12	0
On your tail	Gollum	12	-25

Table 14.1. Example of a personalized leaderboard report.

Duration

Even by changing the identity and the scope, there is still a risk of de-motivation through stagnation. Just as in any race, leaderboards start out exciting as people jockey for position right out of the gate, but as time passes, people start to settle into their rankings. Picture a long distance auto race in which there tends to be very few changes of the top 10 positions as the race plods on. The top 10 participants usually stay in the top 10 because a race is a cumulative effort and once a car falls behind it can become mathematically impossible to catch up without one of the leaders making a critical mistake. But what if the race started over every 20 laps? Short-term leaderboards are a solution that puts everyone back at the starting line, giving people a chance to be in a different rank every so often. Running long-term, cumulative leaderboards locks people into a general rank location on the board. Resetting the leaderboard periodically can give more students a chance to get into that top 10, regardless of past performance.

Relativity

Cumulative point displays are another cause of leaderboard stagnation. If a student falls behind in the rankings it's incredibly difficult to catch up. One way to get around this is to display relative growth instead of cumulative points. To accomplish this, a teacher could choose to display a growth percentage for the week (see Table 14.2). This could give struggling students an advantage in the rankings since their weekly growth could be calculated out to be a higher percentage of their cumulative score. If teachers are using leaderboards to encourage continued effort and growth, they should also be rewarding and displaying growth percentages.

GROWTH RANK	AVATAR NAME	% GROWTH	POINTS THIS WEEK	LEVEL
1	Scotty	+12%	+25	7
2	Kirk	+8%	+50	12
3	Spock	+7%	+30	10

Table 14.2. Example of a leaderboard used to display student growth.

Choice

Perhaps the most effective modification for reducing the shaming effect of leaderboards is to simply make them optional. I have never posted a leaderboard in my classroom that was mandatory for all students. A leaderboard is motivating to more competitive students. For students who shy away from competition, a leaderboard can be devastating. By making a leaderboard an "opt in" part of the gamified classroom, the teacher simultaneously allows the competitive kids to compete for first place while also finding other ways to engage and motivate students who have no interest in jumping into that fray.

Player Types

Even with these possible modifications, a leaderboard system runs the risk of alienating a portion of the class. Leaderboards are not for everybody. They work best for students who have an interest in the competitive aspect of the gamified classroom. Yet, there are other students in the class who are not driven by competition. What, then, are they driven by? If not to win, why would anyone play a game? To answer these questions, we should look at the types of students, or in this case, players, who inhabit the game environment.

Personal differences in gaming motivation became clear to me during a recent game of Scrabble. I played a seemingly brilliant word—one of those small words that was so tightly entwined with other words that it earned me a lot of points while at the same time blocked any other moves in that general area. I was feeling pretty smug until I noticed my friend's expression. "Why, would you do that?" she asked incredulously. "That doesn't help me at all! I thought we were working together." Right then and there my assumption of why we were playing this game was completely turned upside down. I was under the impression that we were competing. She was of the mind that we were cooperating to make the best words and the best of our time together on a rainy day.

Regardless of what the rules say, games are always at the mercy of their players. I was clearly playing Scrabble with someone who had little patience for ruthless competition, but the utmost regard for fun and friendship. Despite what is written in the rulebook, there is no right way to play Scrabble. Gameplay depends on the objectives and motives of the individual players. As much as I would like credit for this idea, the revelation of player dictated uses for games was introduced decades ago. Richard Bartle (1996) published a paper on player motivations in Multi-User Dungeons, or MUDs for short. MUDs were places in the early days of the internet where users could "dial in" to interact with each other in a game-like, text-based environment. Players could enter written commands to interact with anyone else who was in the dungeon. They could chat, trade, fight, explore, and go on quests among other things. Think *World of Warcraft* meets Microsoft Word.

Bartle was interested in the player behaviors that arose within free-form gaming environments. From his observations, he identified four types of players, or more accurately four types of player behaviors: Gladiators, Achievers, Socializers, and

Explorers (1996). These four quadrants were aligned along two spectrums: Acting (upon) versus interacting (with), and player-centered versus game-centered focus. A Gladiator is a player who imposes their will upon other players regardless of the game objectives. Achievers impose their will upon the challenges the game presents regardless of other players. Explorers are not interested in imposing their will on others or the game itself—they want to interact with the game environment and mechanics to truly discover the game. Socializers forego acting upon the game or others and instead are interested in interacting with the other players in the game. These four player types may seem familiar as they simply describe the different ways in which people approach games. Sometimes we play to challenge ourselves. Sometimes we play to play. Sometimes we play to win. Sometimes we play to stay married.

People are motivated to play games for a multitude of reasons and because of this, they also have varying reactions to any given game mechanic. It would be useful then to examine the concept of a leaderboard through the lens of each player type to consider how different players react to the kind of feedback that a leaderboard provides. Even though player type theory has recently evolved as more research has been done on the topic of gamification, it will be enough to use Bartle's original, simple, four-type model to explore leaderboard effectiveness.

Leaderboards for Gladiators

When thinking about the player type that would most likely be engaged by a leaderboard, the mind naturally snaps to Gladiators, the true competitors. These players are why leaderboards exist. Regardless of actual game progress, leaderboards let everyone know who was slain by whom. This is the ultimate motivator for the killer player type, since they are driven by direct competition with other players in the game.

Other player types, however, have varied reactions to a leaderboard system. I have found the less competitive types, like the Explorer and Socializer, are less interested in the rankings and run the highest risk of being demotivated by a traditional leaderboard. While a leaderboard may be an excellent feedback system for the Gladiator player type, other types of players may benefit from different feedback systems.

Badges and Levels for Achievers

The Achiever is driven by getting credit where credit is due. Achievers like to know that they've tackled challenges and like everyone else to know it as well.

Achievers can be motivated by the leaderboard to a certain degree, but only in the sense that it shows how much they've accomplished. However, the leaderboard lacks the specificity to truly give Achievers credit for their deeds. For this reason, an ideal form of feedback for the Achiever player type is a badging system. Badging is a common practice in gamification which involves the awarding of small tokens, either digital or physical, to celebrate specific accomplishments made by the player. Eventually each player will have a collection of badges that will be uniquely theirs which they can show off and compare to others' collections. The Girl Scouts and Boy Scouts of America have been perfecting this practice for years as witnessed by the proudly displayed merit badges on their uniforms. Badges feed an Achiever's need for recognition by acknowledging the individual feats of the player, putting them on display for all to see.

Another feedback mechanism that works well for Achievers is a leveling system based on experience points(XP). For each task a student completes, they earn XP, which helps them advance through a series of milestones indicated by either a numbered level or a titled rank. Much like an enlistee advancing through the ranks of the military, a student's increasing rank and title becomes a source of pride as it reflects the sum of their accomplishments. Usually these ranks are paired with the theme of the game. For example, in a fantasy themed game a player may start out as "peasant" and advance through the ranks of "squire" and "knight" to finally earn the level of "hero" or even "dragon slayer." When it comes to motivating Achievers, both leveling and badging work well to ensure that the Achiever player type can admire all that they've accomplished.

Maps for Explorers

The Explorer is driven by discovery, mystery, novelty, and pushing into new territory. A quantified list of rankings might not be the most motivating feedback system for this player type. In the past, I have to provided the Explorers in my class with a learning map, a graphical display of possible learning activities from which they can choose. Learning maps can take on many different forms like that of an actual map, allowing the players to quest through different territories in the imaginary world of the narrative, or as a simple, tiered menu which lays out all possible tasks based on difficulty and subject matter. A learning map not only helps players see their progress through the narrative of the game, it also allows for players to select their own path through the learning objectives at their own pace.

The Explorer types are known for pushing the limits of the game. They may be interested in adding their own paths to the learning map. They may want to create their own challenges to do things that others have not. Harnessing this desire for exploration can improve the game for everyone. Furthermore, Explorer types endeavor to find all the flaws and loopholes inherent in the game system. While at first it may seem irritating to have a student pick apart the game design, remember that all great games need playtesters who will critically examine games for weaknesses—this is how games grow. Leverage the Explorers to do this playtesting—listen to their findings to improve the overall game design.

Guilds for Socializers

The Socializer is less interested in achievements and gameplay, but rather intrigued by working with others to get things done. While this makes the Socializer type less responsive to the competitive overtones of a leaderboard, it makes them very receptive to the collaborative motivators of the guild system. *Guild* is the gaming term for a group of people or team, who bands together to achieve a common goal. All player types can be represented within a guild, but the Socializers are the ones who usually hold the team together. A guild functions best when players can leverage a variety of strengths and skills from the individual members. Since Socializers are motivated by interacting with other players, establishing a guild system based on player interdependence can be highly engaging for them.

While the guild system is technically not a feedback system like leveling, badging or leaderboards, a guild may cause the Socializer type to be influenced by those around them instead of direct game feedback. A Socializer within the guild will get feedback from other members of the team about overall team performance. This is where the concept of a modified leaderboard can enter the picture as a motivator for Socializers. Instead of, or in addition to, individual rankings, the guilds can be ranked. Making a leaderboard collaborative, instead of individualized, puts the progress of the group in the spotlight rather than the rank of the individual (see Table 14.3). Collaborative, team, or guild leaderboards hold

GUILD RANK	GUILD NAME	GUILD POINTS	TOP CONTRIBUTOR
1	USA	457	FDR
2	Russia	436	Stalin
3	Japan	395	Hirohito

Table 14.3. Example of a collaborative leaderboard.

promise for the Socializers in the game—instilling a sense of team while at the same time activating the sense of urgency that a leaderboard brings to a gamified environment.

Hybrid Designing for Player Types

Considering the multitude of approaches to gaming, it seems each player type might need a different feedback mechanism to be appropriately motivated. It might seem necessary to find the types of players present in each classroom to cater to their motivational needs. Identifying the types of students and specifically differentiating their feedback channels is a daunting proposal. Luckily, this isn't required since player types are not clearly defined subsets of people, but rather observed categories of behavior expressed by the players at any given time. For this reason the boundaries between player types are often blurred. A player may exhibit traits of all types, even though a certain type may be more prominently or frequently displayed. Simply put, even though a student may tend to fall into a specific category, students may be different types of players on different occasions. What motivates them during a game can change depending on their current psychological state. Remember that all students are all player types, at least some of the time.

It would be foolish to assume that using a leaderboard as the sole system of gamified feedback would be effective in motivating any student at all times, let alone all students at all times. The most effective way to cover all the player types is to design a gamified system which includes multiple measures of feedback. All the feedback mechanisms discussed so far—leaderboards, badging, XP leveling, learning maps, and guilds—can work in conjunction. They are not exclusive from each other and function better when combined. For example, a learning map can set players off on a differentiated journey to accomplish quests for badges; badges can include experience points that can make players level up in their guild rank; and the cumulative guild XP can be recorded on a leaderboard. This scenario simultaneously creates differentiated learning, individual achievement, competition, and cooperation. The more ways a teacher can provide feedback in their gamified setting, the more chance they will have of motivating all player types.

Prioritize Design

Even if a designer packs a game full of feedback mechanisms, it does not mean that players will be enticed to play. Nobody chooses to drop that first quarter into an arcade game simply because it has a leaderboard. While feedback systems contribute to players wanting to keep playing, what initially motivates players to play a game is intriguing game design. The same applies to a gamified classroom. When it comes to player motivation, even the fanciest feedback mechanisms pale in comparison to a well-designed challenge structure driven by a compelling storyline.

Consider the dashboard on a car. It's an incredibly useful display since it's a simplified collection of feedback systems for the vehicle. There are several gauges and lights which indicate fuel level, current speed, engine rotations, fuel efficiency, and total distance. Each one individually has an important function, yet none of them would be wholly sufficient in isolation. Multiple methods of feedback help form a better picture of what is currently happening in the car. Think about a leaderboard as just one gauge on the game dashboard that helps students get where they're going.

As useful as a dashboard might be, the vehicle would not go anywhere without all the engineering that actually propels the car when the driver steps on the accelerator. Seeing the dashboard light up is hardly the primary motivator for sliding the key into the ignition. Usually motorists drive because they're trying to get somewhere, like the donut shop before it closes. Without a carefully designed vehicle and an actual desire to head to a destination, the dashboard will collect dust. In a gamified classroom, the student is the driver; the well-designed narrative, experiences, and activities are the car; and the regularly updated display of feedback mechanisms, like badges and learning maps, is the dashboard. When thinking about planning a gamified lesson, first give students an awesome destination. Then design the experiences that will help them get there. Even though this makes the leaderboard and other feedback mechanisms feel less important, it doesn't mean that they should be overlooked. Just as with the fuel gauge, even though it's a very small part of the entire system, it had better function properly or there could be grave consequences.

When gamification is done right, feedback systems take a backseat to the lesson plan. If a task is truly engaging for a student, they partake in the task for the sake of learning, not because of the anticipated grade. My advice for planning a gamified classroom is to start by designing a variety of tasks that will inherently appeal to the various types of player motivations. Make a sampler platter of competitive opportunities, daunting challenges, cooperative activities, and exploratory experiences to satisfy the hunger of all students in the setting. This idea isn't groundbreaking since it's just what great teachers already do. Gamification is just sound teaching repackaged into a game to unlock a higher level of student engagement and ownership.

Carefully crafted, a leaderboard can work in conjunction with other feedback mechanisms to reinforce a motivating gamified learning experience for your students. Conversely, when used carelessly, a leaderboard threatens to harm the motivation of large portions of your class. Decide to use a leaderboard only if it will do more good than harm. Focus on quality learning experiences and student need first. Then, carefully choose game mechanics that will support and amplify your learning environment. In short, teach well and game on.

References

Abramson, L. Y., Seligman, M. E., & Teasdale, J. D. (1978). Learned helplessness in humans: critique and reformulation. *Journal of abnormal psychology, 87*(1), 49.

Bartle, R. (1996). Hearts, clubs, diamonds, spades: Players who suit MUDs. *Journal of MUD research, 1*(1), 19.

Burgers, C., Eden, A., van Engelenburg, M. D., & Buningh, S. (2015). How feedback boosts motivation and play in a brain-training game. *Computers in Human Behavior, 48*, 94-103.

Geisel, T. (1950). *Yertle the Turtle*. New Yorkm, NY: Random House.

Kluger, A. N., & DeNisi, A. (1996). The effects of feedback interventions on performance: An historical review, a meta-analysis, and a preliminary feedback intervention theory. *Psychological Bulletin, 119*(2), 254.

Nicholson, S. (2013). Exploring gamification techniques for classroom management. *Games+ Learning+ Society*, 9.

Ryan, R. M., & Deci, E. L. (2000). Intrinsic and extrinsic motivations: Classic definitions and new directions. *Contemporary Educational Psychology, 25*(1), 54-67.

15

Plugged into Learning with Digital Badges
> Making Learning Fun and Effective

By ANGELA ELKORDY

2 Digital Citizen. Students recognize the rights, responsibilities and opportunities of living, learning and working in an interconnected digital world, and they act and model in ways that are safe, legal and ethical.

5 Computational Thinker. Students develop and employ strategies for understanding and solving problems in ways that leverage the power of technological methods to develop and test solutions.

Gamification for Instruction and Assessment

Most of us play digital games, but don't think about how they work. They are fun and engaging, drawing us into spending significant amounts of time solving puzzles and challenges. Successful games apply key tenets of learning and motivational theories which is why game elements and strategies are so successful at maintaining deep engagement and learning. Gamification is the process of leveraging game-based components like badges or achievements, leaderboards, rewards, and strategies like challenge, choice, and competition for enhanced learning outside of the game environment. Game-based learning is learning using games, digital or otherwise, in content areas to reach target learning objectives.

Today's learners have grown up playing digital games on personal devices like iPads and smartphones, as well as computer-based video games like the Mario series, *Minecraft* and console-based systems including Wii, Xbox and Playstation. Rewards, achievements, and recognitions—often taking the form of digital badges—can be leveraged by educators to create excitement and clarity around learning in their classrooms.

Learning Is Fun Together: Online Cultures

A prominent activity of early internet use was the formation of social or affinity groups around a vast array of topics like politics, support communities, fan fiction, and so on; the list is endless. There is a massive number of participants in multiplayer, online, and role-playing games, as well as online learners and members of professional groups. A defining characteristic of these groups is the sharing of information to connect, inform, share, and transfer knowledge, all of which results in creating and cultivating *social capital*, or the building of identity within social networks. A distinctive trait of these affinity groups, where individuals form groups along similar interests or passions, is participation in these knowledge networks, hence, the description of "participatory cultures" (Jenkins et al., 2009).

Today, more than ever, young people are very active in online participatory cultures, and participation in these networks has been woven into the fabric of how they learn. Young people frequently engage in consuming, producing, and sharing digital content (e.g., videos, writing, media) through Snapchat, Facebook, Twitter, and Instagram. In the process, they're *hanging out*, engaging in discussion, sharing information, music, gaming strategies, and organizing meetings or events. Digital activism, in which teens and youth are heavily engaged, is made possible by the existence of these social media networks. In the context of a modern learning and digital badging discussion, it's important to note the importance of social networks and interaction to today's learners. In large part, the value of a digital badge is conferred by the communities in which it's used—its target audiences are these kinds of youth-driven online cultures.

What Are Digital Badges?

At its most basic level, a digital badge can be described as an *image file with attachments*, including programming code or *metadata* with descriptive information including the organization or individual who issued the badge, expiry date (if pertinent), date of issue, and to whom it was issued. This metadata can also reference external standards, like Common Core State Standards (CCSS), Next Generation Science Standards (NGSS), as well as other standards developed by professional organizations. In addition, details like the badge tasks or criteria may be included to describe how the badge was earned.

Educators on all levels are particularly interested in *open* digital badges, which adhere to technical standards around metadata and display information, making them sharable across wide contexts and different social media. Open badges, when earned, can be collected in "digital backpacks" owned by individuals who can then decide which badges to share, and with whom. Open digital badges have been developed and championed by Mozilla, an organization which also supports a free digital backpack initiative (**openbadges.org/earn/**).

Digital badges are symbols of participation, inclusion, achievement, or accomplishment. The digital variety of badges shares some similarities with the Girl Scouts and Boy Scouts of America badges of the pre-digital age, and have a long history as symbols of achievement in non-gaming environments—since Roman times!

Like scout badges, digital badges have criteria which must be successfully met to earn the badge; the value of the badge is conferred by the members of its communities; and digital badges communicate accomplishments. A digital badge exists entirely online and permits badge earners to share them with numerous audiences, simultaneously, via digital means like social media, online portfolios, web sites whereas a scout badge may only be physically viewed by a local audience.

In digital games, whether computer-based or linked online, badges represent the achievement of something specific, like the completion of mandatory tasks to advance to the next level, or to earn privileges, supplies or special tools (health, wealth, income), or rewards (see Figure 15.1). The accumulation of badges allows us to challenge ourselves and compare our progress to others. Interestingly, badges function in much the same way regardless of context—they serve as *boundary objects*—meaning they traverse boundaries of context, working similarly in different situations. For example, there are many types of games with completely different objectives (i.e., to match three similar objects, to outrun a pursuer, to jump over and through obstacles), and yet we seem to intuitively understand that the ultimate goal is to advance through several levels by accomplishing various tasks and, in the process, be awarded digital badges or *achievements*.

Figure 15.1.
Sample badge.

In games, badges are a sign of successfully accomplishing level-appropriate criteria—the specific tasks may vary based on context. In learning contexts, one of the advantages—and disadvantages—is that badges, criteria and value can vary with context. For example, the *Visible Thinker* badge could be awarded to a third grade student for responses in class, to an eighth grader for articulating a pre-algebra solution or an in-service teacher for sharing reasoning for best practices in teaching metacognitive skills. As with any assessment tool, the value of digital badges is largely conferred and conveyed by the community of learners or practice. Sharing the criteria in a transparent way (i.e., when viewers click on the badge), is a strength of the digital badge.

Badges for Learning

Learning is an any-time, anywhere activity, occurring spontaneously in the context of a digitally-mediated and facilitated world (Fontichiaro & Elkordy, 2013). Learning happens in the classroom, in formal contexts, but also in informal contexts through conversations and online learning, and in libraries, museums, and parks. A learning ecology or interconnected system of digital badges has been proposed to recognize and communicate achievement in a variety of learning contexts. Digital badges are created, displayed, and stored online. They can be implemented as micro-credentials to convey skills acquisition and academic achievement with transparency (Acclaim, 2013). By creating digital badge tasks or criteria, knowledge and skills can be articulated and measured in a new way to include an expanded concept of learning—one which embraces and honors students' learning out of and inside the classroom.

Badges as Motivational Tools

At the right level of challenge, games engage us to connect deeply with content by creating a state of *flow*, a state of deep concentration where participants are completely immersed and engaged in an activity. It's a state in which people are so involved in an activity, that nothing else seems to matter except for resolving the challenge at hand. The flow state is an optimal state of intrinsic motivation (Csíkszentmihályi, 1990), the kind of motivation needed by game participants to get to the next level, or learners to figure out an instructional puzzle.

By understanding how game elements work to create a state of flow, teachers can use these strategies for teaching in their own contexts. Drawing upon theories of motivation, researchers Malone and Lepper (1987) created a classification scheme of game-based elements which "make learning fun." Teachers may recognize some of these motivational elements—like individual challenge, goal setting, curiosity, choice, and performance feedback or interpersonal motivators, like cooperation, competition and recognition—functioning at various times, in their classrooms. In game-based learning, these elements are combined and leveraged through purposeful application, weaving instructional content into games. In gamification, components of games, like leaderboards, achievements, and recognitions (i.e., digital badges), are used in educational or training settings.

Digital badges can incorporate many of these elements to implement strategies familiar to young learners and to leverage the motivational and learning theories at work behind the badge.

Badges as Teaching Tools

Digital badges can be earned for completing specific criteria or tasks which means they can be designed for competency learning, mastery learning of defined skill or knowledge sets (see Figure 15.2). Digital badges can be aligned with the CCSS or other standards, and through purposeful design and badge criteria, a levelled series of badges, can scaffold and spiral learning along a learning trajectory. Clear criteria for learning targets, particularly in sets of levelled badges, can demystify the learning process for students because of their transparency. The extent of learning becomes *visible*. Badge criteria can be very specific and granular, or flexible enough to evidence learning of skill sets or dispositions which are not effectively measured by other means. For example, leadership skills, the ability to converse about a market visit in Arabic, or other performance tasks like design thinking, can be articulated and documented with evidence using digital badges.

Importantly, digital badges provide practical frameworks for differentiation of content, processes, and products of learning. Students can work on badges of different levels, and with flexibility in learning products, and continuing trajectories, differentiation is streamlined. Learners are provided choice in how to demonstrate learning. Instead of earning a grade, they must demonstrate a certain level of competency, or mastery, or learning tasks to earn a digital badge.

Badges as Assessment Tools

Digital badges are earned for completing specific criteria or tasks which means they can be used as a flexible assessment system—for both formative and summative assessment. Badges can augment the process of the assessment of learning and provide feedback by creating a continuum or bridge between formal and informal environments. In implementing a system of visible, incremental levels of expectations,

Figure 15.2. Ways to utilize badges as teaching tools.

digital badges can support positive assessment practices which are formative in nature and support students through detailed feedback (see Figure 15.3).

Because criteria in digital badges can be used to accommodate diverse products of learning, they can be used to personalize learning, by providing choice, autonomy, and challenge at each learner's capability. In the classroom context, discussions around digital badges can foster friendly inter-personal competition as well as cooperation through feedback and collaboration. When used to support a performance assessment, digital badges can entice learners to connect their out-of-school, interest-driven learning with inquiry and problem solving in the classroom context. For example, when encouraged to do so, many kids will use sophisticated skills in digital and social media to complete a task like giving a position presentation on climate change or gathering poll data regarding teen activities in local politics.

At times, when discussing digital badges, it's often asked if they will or should replace traditional grading schemes. As the interest grows in competencies and ways in which to apply knowledge (versus simply reflecting it back on tests), this is a compelling question—particularly as badges can be used to describe distinct competencies which may transfer among various domains. However, for the foreseeable future, digital badges will most likely be used to supplement traditional grading schemes. In fact, digital badges can be integrated into existing assessment frameworks.

Figure 15.3. Badges as assessment tools.

Badges for Lifelong Learning

When assessment is student centered, students can gauge and self-regulate their own learning. These processes foster important characteristics of successful lifelong and life-wide learners, like the development of metacognition (thinking about thinking).

In other words, by providing students the means to assess themselves against the learning objectives, they move faster towards mastery and productive learning routines and habits.

When educators use digital badges to promote interest-driven, personalized learning, perhaps even providing a place for students to incorporate learning from non-school contexts, they promote the rich engagement with content necessary for deep learning (see Figure 15.4). They provide tools for learners to understand how learning works through development of their metacognition—and in using digital badges, educators leverage the successful principles of learning and motivation science beyond the engagement of games.

Badges for Learner Identity

For some learners, particularly students who face challenges in traditional learning contexts, like gaps in prior knowledge, language or reading barriers or special needs, it can be difficult for them to view themselves as successful at learning. By providing evidence of achievements, digital badges can foster a positive learning identity that increases student confidence and belief in their own capacities. Badges build upon a strengths model because badges aren't taken away—they are simply not earned, unlike traditional grading schemes based upon a deficit model (see Figure 15.5). A digital badge collection can reinforce a positive self-concept which is so important for the future success of all types of learners.

Digital Badges as Teaching and Assessment Tools

Digital badges are flexible tools for teaching, learning and assessment. They're boundary objects, representing similar concepts (e.g., achievements or awards) in diverse contexts. For example, a digital badge could be awarded for completion of criteria in plant science or completion of a math assignment. Despite the different contexts, there are however, some basic principles of good and bad badging practices.

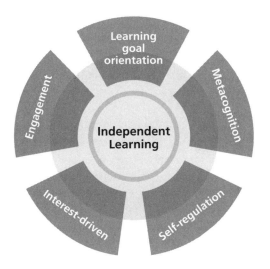

Figure 15.4. Outcomes of utilizing badges for independent learning.

Figure 15.5. Ways that badges foster positive learning experiences.

Poor Badging Practices

> ***Too easy to earn.*** While there is a value to demonstrating participation—for example, in cultivating community—by and large, people aren't very excited about getting badges just for "showing up." Badges that are too easy to earn or acquire tend not to be highly *valued* by an individual or the learning community at large.

> ***Too hard to earn.*** A strength of digital badging systems is the capacity to scaffold learning by deconstructing tasks into their components. If badge tasks or criteria are not within learners' zone of proximal development, or are inappropriately sequenced or scaffolded, learners will not be motivated to earn them.

> ***Badge issuer.*** The credibility of the badge credential rests upon the credibility of its issuer.

> ***Means of assessment.*** If similar performance standards and expectations are not being applied to potential earners, learners will lose interest in attaining the badge.

> ***Poor badging criteria.*** If the badge criteria are ambiguous, too difficult, or too numerous, students will lose motivation.

> ***Delayed recognition.*** In order to be effective for motivating students, earned badges must be distributed promptly.

Good Badging Practices

> **Well-defined badging criteria.** Badges with clear goals and objectives motivate students.

> **Encouraging choice and fostering creativity.** Build in several options of learning products for students to demonstrate mastery of learning objectives.

> **Culturally responsive badging practices.** While some students may thrive on public sharing of digital badges, others may feel anxious, perceive this as bragging, or undesirable for other reasons. This doesn't mean your students don't like to earn achievements, just that they may not like to share them widely—know your students' preferences.

> **Designing and implementing in teams.** Digital badges can be designed as a kind of common assessment.

> **Link learning artifacts or evidence of learning.** A significant benefit of digital badges to recognize and communicate learning lies in their capacity to directly link evidence of learning.

Digital badges can be an effective instructional strategy to motivate students to learn (see Figure 15.6). Using carefully-designed digital badges, teachers can empower students to have more agency over their own learning, in the game-familiar currency of achievements. The widening, artificial chasm between out-of-school learning and the formal school context can effectively be bridged by encouraging learners to incorporate knowledge and skills gained through interest-learning *on their own time*. In addition, by offering a selection or choice of

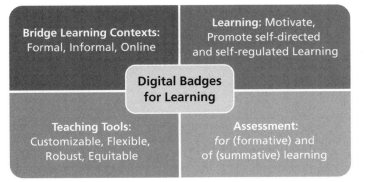

Figure 15.6. Ways digital badges support learning.

learning products or ways to demonstrate learning, learners are more engaged in the process and products of learning.

In recognizing, measuring and communicating effectively, digital badges can cast light onto previously unknown skills acquisition by articulating the learning—by making it *visible* to teachers, parents, peers and the community.

Digital Badge Advantages

A great deal of learning in classrooms is neither measured, nor communicated. It's hard to assess and communicate growing skills in inter-personal skills, for example, persistence or empathy. A traditional grading schema does not convey information about specific skills—what does a B grade in Spanish or music or literature really mean? In making learning *visible* through badge criteria, it's possible to describe the acquisition of specific knowledge and skills which may not be measured or recognized, particularly through standardized testing. Digital badges can evidence growth.

Teachers see the potential for leveraging digital badges in the classroom for scaffolding and differentiating instruction, for motivating students, and to teach skills or competencies in ways which transfer easily to other contexts or domains (see

Figure 15.7. Benefits of badging for teachers.

Figure 15.7). When learning is made visible, learners can see their progress and have clarity around steps to move forward.

A digital badge system can also help in creating strong communities of learners within the classroom and develop groups based on learner interests. A vibrant community of learners working towards attainable goals will motivate its members to collaborate, cooperate (particularly through sharing ideas and feedback), and foster friendly competition.

Teachers like how digital badges can engage students in their own learning in a competency-based manner, since skills and knowledge transfer is streamlined (see Figure 15.8). Most of all, educators like the flexibility of digital badges as a tool to motivate learners to persist in learning tasks.

Leveraging Learning with Digital Badges

The use of digital badges for learning can provide unique affordances to learners. Diverse knowledge and skills sets may be effectively evaluated and communicated and individualized pathways of interest-motivated learning may be pursued. Learning from non-school contexts can be recognized and valued, and in an engaging, familiar and learner-centric manner. Students who may struggle to demonstrate academic achievement in formal learning environments may be more motivated to learn when learning pathways include self-motivated learning behaviors and preferences.

Figure 15.8.
Sample badge.

Kids face challenges in equity of opportunity in education—challenges which persist into workplace and economic opportunities. A digital badge ecosystem provides opportunities for learners to develop and demonstrate competencies in a variety of contexts. The contexts of learning are neither bound by location nor resources.

As the chasm between interest and classroom learning grows, students have become increasingly disengaged. Digital badges can be used to create personalized learning spaces to re-engage learners and learning can be fun.

Resources

Edutopia Game-based Learning: **www.edutopia.org/blogs/beat/ game-based-learning**

K12 badge twitter chat: **flipboard.com/@noahgeisel7/badge-chat-f7a3sm21y**

References

Acclaim. (2013). Open badges for higher education. Retrieved from http://www. pearsonlearningsolutions.com/blog/wp-content/uploads/2013/12/Open-Badges-for-Higher-Education.pdf

Csikszentmihalyi, M. (1990). *Flow: The psychology of optimal experience.* New York, NY: Harper & Row.

Elkordy, A. (2016). Development and Implementation of Digital Badges for Learning Science, Technology, Engineering and Math (STEM) Practices in Secondary Contexts: A Pedagogical Approach with Empirical Evidence. In *Foundation of Digital Badges and Micro-Credentials,* 483-508. New York, NY: Springer International Publishing.

Fontichiaro, K., & Elkordy, A. (2013). From stars to constellations: Digital badges can chart growth. *Learning and Leading with Technology, 41*(4), 12-15.

Ito, M., Gutiérrez, K., Livingstone, S., Penuel, B., Rhodes, J., Salen, K., Watkins, S. C. (2013). *Connected learning: An agenda for research and design.* Irvine, CA: Digital Media and Learning Research Hub. Retrieved from http://dmlhub.net/sites/default/files/ConnectedLearning_report.pdf

Jenkins, H., Purushotma, R., Weigel, M., Clinton, K., & Robison, A. J. (2009). *Confronting the challenges of participatory culture: Media education for the 21st century.* Boston, MA: MIT Press.

Malone, T. & Lepper (1987). Making Learning Fun: A Taxonomy of Intrinsic Motivations for Learning. In Snow, R. & Farr, M. J. (Ed), Aptitude, Learning, and Instruction (Vol. 3). Hillsdale, NJ: Lawrence Erlbaum Associates, Publishers.

16

Leveled Up!

> Tips for Recognizing Student Achievements with Badges

By MJ LINANE

ISTE Standards for Students

2 Digital Citizen. Students recognize the rights, responsibilities and opportunities of living, learning and working in an interconnected digital world, and they act and model in ways that are safe, legal and ethical.

5 Computational Thinker. Students develop and employ strategies for understanding and solving problems in ways that leverage the power of technological methods to develop and test solutions.

The Forgettable Classroom

One of my suitemates in college was a level 12 gnome mage. Well, at least he pretended to be in the computer game, *World of Warcraft*. *World of Warcraft* was released in November 2004, and he had played for only a couple of weeks on his custom-built gaming computer. I happened to walk by his room one day and saw him playing. I wanted to know more about it because it was unlike any game I had seen before.

I had played first-person shooters before but *World of Warcraft* was my first true encounter with a massive multiplayer online role-playing game (MMORPG): a game where millions of people from across the globe progress their fantasy character in a virtual world. Now, my roommate was only a level 12. The character levels in *World of Warcraft* went has high as 60, so a level 12 gnome mage is the equivalent to an infant in skills and abilities.

There was something enticing to me about his character and that world. Anyone could join, start at level one and slowly progress their characters around others who were trying to accomplish the same. We were individual players, motivated by individual goals, playing in a communal space. Working alone was possible but many worked together in groups called guilds. Players chose their character's race, appearance and skill set. A player's character was theirs—a representative of themselves. In many ways, the character became a sort of manifestation of the player. If a person wanted to be helpful, they chose a healing role, if they wanted to mainly attack others, they chose a character class whose main role was to battle others.

As the player completed quests and activities in the game, they gained experience points that were tracked at the bottom of the screen. Players always knew what the goal was, and when they were about to get to the next skill level.

As they gained experience, players progressed in levels, gained new skills, and became more powerful. All of this was reflected in the powers players used in the game, and the appearance of their character that became more and more unique. Don't let me undersell it—a level 60 character looks awesome. A level 60 character has all of the best armor, wields the best weapons, and has the most powers. I'll admit that I played *World of Warcraft* for some time in college, and I loved it. Others did too. At the height of its popularity, *World of Warcraft* had 12 million monthly subscribers. (McDougall, 2010). Since then, many other games have tried to copy the success and community of *World of Warcraft*. These games have met with varying success but more importantly, they've offered gamers more opportunities to build virtual identities and progress their lives in virtual worlds.

Like *World of Warcraft*, I felt college gave me a sense of progression in both skills and knowledge. More so than high school, I felt like I was going somewhere. I had a plan. I knew what my goal was. Homework assignments were quests to me and each one meant I was on the verge of "leveling up." When I left college and started teaching in 2004, I naively expected teaching to mimic college and games. I expected daily life would be filled with a sense of progression and the goals would be clear. I was wrong.

I was lucky enough to land a job teaching United States history in a suburb about 10 miles north of Boston, MA. To prepare, I had completed my student teaching while in college. I had student taught in a high school United States history course so I wasn't completely ignorant to the realities of teaching. But, no one can really prepare for becoming a classroom teacher. I remember being incredibly busy my first year teaching. Most days I was trying to teach myself the content and then prepare lessons. I was so involved with *what* I was teaching that I didn't think about *how* I was teaching.

My initial teaching style could best be described as *traditional.* Unfortunately, tradition nearly ended my career. I thought my purpose was to make students experts on history—to teach them to memorize the facts. That's what I did. Every assessment asked students to repeat facts. Weekly quizzes consisted of students identifying and matching vocabulary from memory. Maybe once in a while I would let them use a 3x5 index card as a "cheat sheet." Every two weeks, I gave students a unit tests that had multiple choice questions and an open response questions. How did I recommend students prepare? *"Memorize,"* I would tell them, "it's easy!" Make some flashcards. I even gave out bonus points for students when they turned in their flashcards before a test. I did this same cycle for five years. Occasionally I would add in a research project but, usually, students could set their watch by my predictable assessments. After five years, I was done; burnt out. By 2013, I dreaded correcting one more multiple choice question. I loathed reading another open response that didn't have a single paragraph break in it. Looking back, I shouldn't have been so angry about my students' writing skills. I rarely taught essay writing—I taught memorization. Reflecting on my disillusionment, it wasn't the predictability that got to me. It was when I realized that my focus was on memorizing facts, and that was meaningless to students.

During the winter of 2012, my high school history department conducted an insightful, yet completely unscientific study. We wanted to know how much historical content our present and past history students actually remembered from our courses. We wanted to see if sophomores currently learning United States history remembered more than the juniors on an objective assessment. We used 40 multiple choice questions from a sophomore final exam, and gave them to the sophomores, juniors, and freshman as a control group. The results were unexpected. Students in all three grades scored between 27 and 36%. Freshman scored the lowest with 27%, sophomores the highest with 36%, and juniors 32%. As a department, we couldn't do much with those shocking results besides discuss and reflect on how we could improve. It made sense that sophomores who had most recently learned the material scored the highest, but I expected juniors to perform much better. And most shockingly, freshman scored at just over 25%

without a single lesson in United States history since fifth grade. I wondered what was it all for. I spent thousands of hours trying to help students memorize history only to be defeated by time. With enough time, students forgot almost every fact I taught them.

I used to start class by asking, "What did we learn last class?" Sometimes I asked for responses verbally or written down. Many times, a student or two responded with a name or a concept but, for the most part, many didn't remember. I've asked in April about a topic we covered in September, and students simply didn't remember. They would say that it was "too long ago," or "I can't remember that far back." But ask a student about a time they scored a goal on the soccer field or won a gymnastics, band, or dance competition, and they can tell you all sorts of things—about the day it happened, the time, the weather, and who was watching them. A moment like that means something to a student. Students get the same feeling from playing video games, from competing, and achieving their life's goals and ambitions. No wonder students forgot my class. I gave them nothing to mark their achievements, nothing to indicate goals or progress. In 2013, I decided to turn my classroom on its head. I was going to help students not just learn but level up. I wanted to give them a sense of progress and pride, not just tools to memorize history, but the personal motivation to excel by learning lessons from history. I started by celebrating student achievements.

Do Badges Actually Work?

Students want more engagement than what an average class can offer. Students are constantly distracted by pressures other than class: cell phones, friends, parents, sports. Those distractions are powerful lures for students since at the heart of it, learning is hard work. It's easy for educators to feel powerless or marginalized in the lives of their students. Yet there are ways that educators can dramatically increase the interest of students.

One way that's proven to increase engagement is by giving students a sense of mastery. An easy way to recognize mastery is to recognize achievement. This chapter is here to help you get started recognizing student achievement to engage students.

Traditional grades are a powerful motivator for students. Yet, for many students it is not enough because grades are only extrinsic motivators. Grades become a tool of disengagement once students fail to see continued success. Additionally, grades only reward academic behaviors and only when students are performing at 100%,

100% of the time. This can keep many students from being recognized for their great work.

The way I chose to increase student engagement was to gamify my classes. I did this to take the pressure off performance, and to offer chances for students to be recognized. We can teach students to be intrinsically motivated by offering them purpose, a chance for mastery, and to both offer and recognize student autonomy. I try to do all three by recognizing students through achievements and representative badges.

You may be skeptical about giving out badges. But consider that militaries across the world give out badges and recognize achievements as a part of their toolkit of motivation. If they can be used to recognize great acts of bravery and sacrifice, why are educators above recognizing outstanding acts by their students?

As educators, we need every tool to be in our toolkit to help our students succeed. We want our students to feel motivated and accomplished, and to love learning. You can accomplish all three by stopping to celebrate your students.

To help you get started quickly, I have put together some of my best tips and strategies.

Recognize Greatness

We need to consider what the point of badges are in the first place. They offer a way for individuals to be recognized for their accomplishments. In this case, students are receiving them for doing something awesome in your class.

The reality for me is that some of the badges I give out to students recognize achievements few will ever perform. This is good. You want different levels of badges or achievements for your students. That way there will be some that everyone will have a chance to receive. For instance, I give out one after every unit. These will be common and valueless for most students, but for some, these easy ones might be the only ones they achieve. And for some of our students, simply completing the year is a personal victory.

To get started, make a list of all the most difficult things to achieve in your class. Maybe it's getting three As in a row, maybe it's revising an assignment more than once. Maybe it's more basic, like coming to class every day with the class supplies. Whatever it is that your students have trouble doing consistently, choose the best case scenario. Then make that a badge.

Go Beyond Grades

As educators, our primary goal is to have students learn: learn content, learn skills, learn to be a better person. Unfortunately, most educators think about recognizing achievements that relate to grades. Content is a source, but it doesn't need to be the only one. Think about what type of classroom environment you would like to have, then create the badges or achievements that you would want students to perform. This serves two purposes. First, having two different categories of badges ensures that no one is getting left out from achieving in your class. Everyone loves being recognized for their effort! Second, it allows you to shape your classroom by recognizing and rewarding good behavior. I have badges that recognize when students help each other without me asking. It creates a much more collaborative classroom.

The Medal of Honor is a United States military award that recognizes outstanding acts of valor. There are five branches of the United States military: Army, Navy, Air Force, Coast Guard, and Marine Corp. All branches together have 154 medals and ribbons recognizing those who serve. They range from the Purple Heart for those who are wounded to ribbons for pistol marksmanship. While medals are not the motivation for everyone in the armed forces, the significance of the Medal of Honor is undeniable. It recognizes unique actions of soldiers, and you too can create badges that recognize whatever is unique to your class.

Be Creative

Feel free to be as creative as you want when recognizing students. Creating these new achievements and badges should be fun for you, not additional work. I think I have more fun creating them than I do giving them out.

I teach freshman World History and many students are nervous before their first test. So, I hold a one hour, online, voluntary Q&A. The last time I held a Q&A, about 20 students showed up, so I wanted to recognize their additional effort. The next day, I made an achievement and badge for them. When I named the achievement, I could have called it "Came For Extra Help At Night." Instead I had some fun and called it "Night Owl" and the badge included the picture of an owl. I'll also take my common units throughout the year and make achievements out of them. For instance, the unit on the Russian Revolution became "Hero of the Soviet Union" with the accompanying hammer and sickle.

When creating your first badge, make it simple to link it to the curriculum. If you want a larger theme for the achievements you offer to your students, think about your own life or teaching experiences. I use historical events and themes to make my badges, but your badges don't have to relate to your curriculum. I know a teacher who made his achievements baseball-themed. What a unique and interesting way to engage students, personalize your teaching, and recognize students for their achievements in ways other than grades! Like him, you could create badges on a single theme that you're passionate about.

To get started, ask yourself: what sport, video, or board games have I played? What shows have I watched? What books have I read and liked? What trophies or awards have I received? Consider your background and interests, then try to make that your theme for the class. The badges work a lot better if *you* believe them to be fun, authentic, and important. Take common characters, events, or icons from those experiences and combine them into a theme. As you build your badges, draw upon the theme to make the names and icons.

Display the Badges

One of the most important aspects of badges is their value in recognizing student efforts towards mastery. Making progress towards mastery is a key intrinsic motivator for all humans. Recognizing student efforts towards mastery is something that celebrates individuals and can inspire the class. As an educator, if you want to try and encourage students to earn these achievements, then there must be a way to publicly celebrate them.

Every time I start class, I recognize students who won achievements, and everyone gives them a round of applause. Using a tool or service can make this step easy, but remember that this should not be made into a competitive part of class. Competitiveness will only serve to demotivate. Use it as a way for students to feel proud and accomplished.

Do you have a bulletin board? A learning management system? Your own teacher website? I have known teachers who issue digital badges, physical badges, or both. It's all about what works for you and your students. Remember, recognizing achievements is something to be celebrated. How you display them can be as varied and as creative as the badges themselves. I issue mine digitally using my learning management system. Ultimately, if they are displayed and students can view each other's badges, the achievements are being celebrated.

Badges Can Be Collaborative

Learning is not a solitary act. Why make all your achievements and badges about an individual? I have designed badges that recognize great group work. I have another badge called "Medic" for someone who, unsolicited, willingly helps another student before I can get to them. Another category of badges recognizes when an entire class does something awesome. I have a badge that is given to an entire class if everyone completes every assignment in a term. I have only ever had one class come close. Out of 23 students and 10 graded assignments, only one student missed one assignment for the entire term. I told the class how close they were but not who the student with the missing assignment was. I wanted them to know that the badge was worth striving for. Also, that the badge was something that could be achieved if students supported one another.

Collaborative badges offer students the chance to increase their class solidarity and collaboration but also to decrease the risk of action. Students achieve collaborative badges or not, but they do it together. Because these are badges obtained as a group, it's a good strategy to offer unique badges or achievements to students who wouldn't regularly receive them.

Don't Over-Badge

One of the mistakes many make is to have a badge for everything a student could do. Instead of recognizing a student's efforts, badges then lose their value. Imagine badges as currency—the more badges are issued, the less valuable they become. Strike a balance between recognizing students regularly but not issuing badges every day.

An easy way to avoid over-badging is to plan out when you expect to issue your badges. You will want to try to avoid "badge fatigue." This is when getting a badge just becomes another extrinsic motivator for a student. Teachers want to strike a balance between awarding students badges too often and too infrequently. I usually recommend awarding the entire class an achievement after the completion of studying a unit. This will ensure that every student is receiving recognition often. I see my classes every other day so on average, I award unit completion badges every two to three weeks. I will otherwise plan to distribute unique badges to three to five students every week for various acts. The balance of too many and too few will need to be personalized to you, your students, and your class schedule. A lot the balance comes from trial and error.

Badges Are Neither Carrot nor Stick

A common mistake educators make when they try to recognize students is to make it all about the badges or achievements. Students are smart, and they will be able to pick up on your efforts to manipulate them. If badges are used as a clear tool to get students to complete their homework, then it will be just that: a tool. The whole benefit will be erased. Even worse, studies have shown this to even demotivate people.

You want student achievements and badges to be something that makes students feel good, not used. I recommend staying away from saying "If you do your homework, you'll earn this badge." Instead reward students who maybe complete their homework five times in a row. Look for where your problem areas are in your class and recognize when students do well.

Humans are surprisingly predictable and one of the best books I have read on motivation is Daniel Pink's *Drive: The Surprising Truth About What Motivates Us* (2009). What Pink details is our basic drive by extrinsic or intrinsic motivation. As teachers, we can provide more intrinsic motivation by supporting each of these three motivators: mastery, autonomy, and purpose.

While recognizing achievements may only represent mastery, I also have achievements that recognize autonomy. Students who complete independent "genius hour" or "side quest" activities as a part of a term will receive a badge too. Genius hour activities are independent learning projects by students once all their other work is complete. Students can explore further content within our current unit and create something using their unique talents that helps other students. Students creations have included instructional guides, graphic depictions, infographics, musical performances, animated cartoons, and 3D models. Students that build these additional creations and go beyond the standard assignments receive "The Artisan" badge. It provides a way to recognize those students who surpass expectations for the benefit of others.

There have been a lot of studies done that have shown a negative reaction by students and workers who are forcibly motivated to do well by teachers and bosses. If you find yourself making "if/then" statements, you might be using badges in a way that will do more harm than good and that may result in demotivation.

Badges Can Be Repeatable

Recognizing students doesn't have to turn your classroom into the Academy Awards. Often in our lives there is one award to be won. Only one film can be "Film of the Year," but this model isn't sustainable in education, nor should it be. If you are like me, you encourage your students to set their own personal goals and to work towards their own mastery. And if that's the case, the "one-and-done" style of recognizing achievement won't work for you either. Make your badges repeatable and you'll ensure that all students will be recognized.

For instance, I currently have 37 badges to recognize student achievement throughout the year. All but twelve of those are repeatable. While we think repeating would remove some of the value of the achievement, it doesn't. Every achievement is personal to the student. Each one is valuable, whether earned by someone else or not.

How many times do you want to recognize student achievements? In the 2014-2015 school year, I recognized a total of 1,232 achievements using 32 badges. That year I had 95 students, which means I recognized each student 12.9 times that year on average. Over the course of three years, I have positively recognized thousands of student actions.

Leave Badging Options Open

An easy way to make sure students are regularly being recognized for their efforts is to make some of the badges repeatable and others a mystery. For instance, for the badge called "Medic" students willingly helped another student before I was called on or was able to help. This might be answering an online question or helping a student with an online tool we were using. I made it repeatable because I want to encourage collaboration as the class standard.

I have a running list on Schoology (**schoology.com**) of all the achievements for my classes, but I have a whole category called "Hidden." No badge names, no descriptions, no images. The secret? I have no idea what they are. I keep my options open for when students do something that surprises me. I can create a badge at that very moment.

To design your own badges, first make a list of all the awesome things students could do in your class this year. It might include grades, content, or behavior. Write it all down. Take the most repeated items and think of them as your common badges. The more difficult actions or events might be your uncommon badges. All of these are visible to your students, so they can keep the targets in mind if they want. The actions or events that are the rarest are recognized by your hidden badges.

In June of 2016, in the closing days of the school year, my school received warning of a possible threat. Before the lockdown, I was helping three freshman students with their history project during my planning block. We were just finishing up when the lockdown was announced, we locked the door, pulled the shades, and tucked ourselves into a corner of the room awaiting further instruction. The police patrolling the building outside indicated the gravity of the situation. Luckily, it turned out to be a false alarm. I am not ashamed to admit that I was a little concerned, as were two of the other three freshman students in my classroom. The third freshman was completely calm. I mean calm like an experienced zen master. When I asked if everyone was okay, she reacted, "Yeah, I'm okay. I think we will be okay." That's the type of unexpected bravery that would be worth a hidden achievement. I wanted to create a badge called "Unwavering Courage" for all my students, not to celebrate the situation, but to recognize their calm response to a stressful event. I leave a place for a hidden badge to remind me about the achievement, hoping I will never again have to reveal that particular one.

Creating badges is an effective way to recognize students and to highly motivate them. It doesn't need to turn into a second job. You already have enough to do. Adding different tools to your toolbox can help you create the type of class you want while doing minimal extra work. In some cases, these tools can make your life easier and the students happier by extending the role badges and achievements can play in your classroom.

References

McDougall, J. (2010). *The Media Teacher's Book*. Abigdon, UK: Hodder Education.

Pink, D. H. (2009). *Drive: the surprising truth about what motivates us*. New York, NY: Riverhead Books.

Resources

Classcraft, turn your class into an adventure!: **classcraft.com**

Classdojo classroom communication app: **classdojo.com**

Credly (tools for recognizing acheivement): **credly.com**

Schoology learning management system: **schoology.com**

17

Get the Best (and Avoid the Worst) from Gamification

By SCOTT R. GARRIGAN

What's the Difference Between *Game* and *Gamification*?

Let's start with a story about yourself and how you were originally motivated to learn. How did you learn to speak when you were one year old? Was there a system of points, badges, and leaderboards? You learned to speak to empower yourself, to make yourself understood, to get what you wanted, to learn the rules of the game of communication in your family. As your language skills increased, you leveled up authentically as people accepted you into higher levels of discourse. You

Figure 17.1. One way to look at games and gamification. The intersection represents the holy grail of a true learning game that students love to play and learn at a fantastic pace.

were powerfully motivated by a system that existed since the dawn of language, before games or gamification, before schools (see Figure 17.1).

We discovered that most school-age children, when playing a video game of their choice, can pay attention for hours, will choose harder over easier tasks, and learn new cognitive game skills at a ferocious pace. Some teachers and parents were so alarmed by their children's intense engagement that they blamed video games for poor school performance! But let's take a closer look at games to see how they may be different from school and other activities.

Games have attracted young and old players for millennia. For most of history, life was hard work. In contrast to work, games were fun! Whether they were games of strategy like chess and Go, games of chance like dice and card games, or games of skill like physical sports, great effort was expended for the promise of little tangible reward. A few games were solitary like the aptly-named Solitaire, but most were social to be played with friends.

Games are *Played*

Have you played basketball, Monopoly, chess, *Space Invaders*, *World of Warcraft*, bridge, or *Pokemon Go*? Whether it's a card, board, video, or war game, you *play* the game.

Philosopher George Santayana suggested, "Play is whatever is done spontaneously and for its own sake." This implies that play is *voluntary*. If you must play, it's not play.

Many definitions of *game* incorporate the ideas of *voluntary play* like this one: "A game is a voluntary interactive activity that engages players in challenging, structured activity that can be won or lost." Game designer and author Jesse Schell (2008) knows that games are usually defined by their components. For example, games have rules and goals, they may have conflict, and they can be won or lost. But Schell wants to define the *essence* of a game, and he likes the ideas in Greg Costikyan's definition: a game is "an interactive structure of endogenous meaning that requires players to struggle toward a goal" (Schell, 2008).

Notice that Costikyan begins with *interactivity;* you can't be a passive game player. *Structure* implies rules, and *endogenous* means that *the game's value lies inside itself.* The gameplay may have little to no meaning outside itself; does beating a Boss have meaning outside of the game? And struggle implies *challenge.* We'll come back to these big ideas shortly, but this definition is too abstract for Schell. His simple, elegant definition emphasizes the dominant elements of challenge and play: "A game is a problem-solving activity, approached with a playful attitude" (Schell, 2008).

How Does Motivation in a Game Differ from Gamification?

Why do we play? Because games are fun to play. But exactly what makes games fun? Are there fun ingredients? Around 1980 as kids grew addicted to video games, Tom Malone and his Stanford advisor Mark Lepper wanted to know the answer. "Making Learning Fun" was the eventual title of Malone's dissertation (1987), and it remains a valuable in-depth study of the elements of game fun. Malone and Lepper found four elements that school-age players find intrinsically motivating—elements that make students want to return to play a game again and again: **challenge, curiosity, control,** and **fantasy.** After more than 35 years of continued study, these four elements have withstood the test of time for individual-player games. Let's explore each one since they're central to understanding intrinsic motivation in students.

Intrinsic Motivation

> **Challenge.** Does anyone like to play a game without challenge? Remember the card game Go Fish? It's pure chance, there's no skill involved, and you can't become a better player. Compare Go Fish to *Super Mario Bros.* where each level introduces new skills to learn, and mastering each skill becomes the new challenge. When the skills of one level are mastered, you level up to a harder level with new things to learn. Game players love to challenge themselves whether

they're playing a computer game, a card game, or a sport. The key is that the *player* accepts the challenge as a personal goal, not one imposed by teachers, employers, or parents.

> **Curiosity and Surprise.** Every good game is filled with surprises. In board games like Monopoly, you are surprised every time you pick a card. Computer games surprise you at every turn, and new surprises await in every level. Games use chance and random, unpredictable events to keep the surprises coming. Every player is curious about what the next surprise will be.

> **Control.** From the first choice to play a game or not, to the last choice playing again or not, the player is in control. Some games give the player control over the game's challenge by allowing a choice of levels or choice of difficulty. In others, players choose their own avatar. Even in a modern, adult-oriented game like *Ingress*, players first must choose their team. Similarly, choices in an educational activity gives students agency, the feeling that they're empowered to choose and have the responsibility to make wise choices. Each of these makes the player or student feel they're in control of the activity, game, or sport. They can even stop whenever they want.

> **Fantasy.** The most playful elements of many games involve the fantasy storyline provided by the game. In the Mario series of platform games, we play a hard-working, happy plumber in the Mushroom Kingdom often rescuing Princess Peach. In *World of Warcraft*, we choose our avatar from an array of wizards and warriors. And we play as warriors in nearly every military game. We are charged with protecting earth from space invaders. Even in chess, there's the fantasy of protecting your king and queen using your knights and castles. Sports teams and their mascots often take fantasy names like the Giants, Astros, and Pirates. Young children may identify with the fantasy characters they play as and play against. Players give themselves names that support the fantasy of the characters they play.

But something is missing from this list. So many of our favorite games, from cards and sports, to massive multiplayer online games, are played with others. So many games are social engagements, and Malone and Lepper (1987) identified three additional factors of interpersonal motivation that help to make games fun to play: **cooperation**, **competition**, and **recognition**.

> **Cooperation.** Think of team sports like baseball and soccer compared to more individual sports like tennis and swimming. Similarly in computer games, there are individual games and team games. One of the best know team games is

World of Warcraft where success is determined by the different strengths of individual team members as they work together as a group. Successful team players are responsible for carrying out their tasks just as a baseball pitcher has a specific role to play for his team. Students are social learners as well as individual learners. Even young children recognize the value of cooperative roles as their favorite superheroes work together in teams to fight evil.

> **Competition.** Children and adults love to play competitive games and sports. Why? An obvious answer might be that we all want to win, and we may think that winning means coming in first or having the highest score. Young children, however, love to play competitive games without keeping score—it's just fun to measure your own skill or self-efficacy relative to others. But, does that mean there is only one winner and everyone else is a loser? We can also compete against ourselves and our former high score. Everyone who reaches a certain milestone may be a winner. Or, like a marathon, there can be one first-place winner, but everyone who crosses the finish line is cheered as a winner just for finishing! Many computer games have leaderboards that show the top scores. A good question would be how much the leaderboard motivates most players when only a few make the top scores.

> **Recognition.** Many of us crave recognition, and sports and movie stars may be the poster children for social recognition. Early teens, in particular, have strong social drives as they crave identity and recognition. We value ourselves in part by how others value. Recognition does require that our work must be visible for others to judge. Schools have to deal with FERPA-style regulations that may require student academic records like scores to be kept confidential, but there are a variety of ways to convey student achievement. Another kind of recognition celebrates the eclectic diversity of students as in an art gallery exhibition or posted work in an open house. Students value their own work more highly when they see others react favorably to it.

Games are *Rewarding*—They Keep on Giving!

Just because most games have scores and levels, some people believe that games are played mostly for the reward of high scores and levels. But imagine you are a tennis player who can choose easy opponents to rack up wins, or your can choose challenging opponents and lose some matches. Most players choose challenge over high score. The idea that players are motivated mostly by high scores is a dangerous assumption. Lots of players find the act of playing to be the most rewarding part of a game. As we saw above, Malone and Lepper identified seven reasons why we play hard, because games embody those elements that elicit intrinsic motivation (see Figure 17.2).

In video games, most players seek to increase their mastery of the game. To do so, they seek increasingly hard challenges. They may play a harder level and fail rather than play an easy level and get a high score. The intrinsic motivators in games are so rewarding that players seek ever-increasing challenges, and they come back to play again and again. How does this compare to gamification?

Gamification Tends to Rely on Extrinsic Motivation

My favorite simple definition of gamification comes from Chris Aviles, a classroom teacher and blogger. Gamification "is the use of game mechanics and elements in nongame contexts. Gamification is taking the game mechanics and elements that kids love about video games and installing them into to your classroom. Your

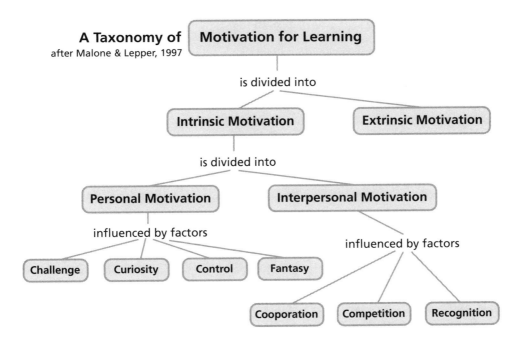

Figure 17.2. Overview of intrinsic motivation factors elicited by games. A challenge for gamification is to incorporate intrinsic motivation factors in a way that students regard them more as a fun game and less like sugar-coated school work.

classroom doesn't use video games, your classroom is a video game" (Aviles, 2016). In those words, Chris suggests gamification can transform a non-game environment into a real game. But his words of installing game mechanics and elements into your classroom are not enough, which is important to understand since the stakes in education are so high. Gamification advocates suggest that ordinary school learning can become as engaging as a popular game through the thoughtful addition of "game elements." But how well does this seductive idea really work? Can we count on it to help our kids learn? Especially our kids who have trouble learning?

Let's compare gamification in education to corporate gamified products. Nike Plus and other fitness programs give points, badges, challenges, and competition to help you reach milestones in your fitness goals. Mint.com does the same thing for personal finance. Ford equips its Fusion Hybrid with "efficiency leaves" on a virtual dashboard plant to foster ecological driving as drivers try to keep the plant healthy.

Corporate gamified initiatives all follow a familiar path:

1. **There's an activity that you want people to do more or better.**
2. **Points are given to reward the desired behavior.**
3. **Badges are given for achieving milestones.**
4. **Leaderboards show how you compare to the top scorers.**

Gamification advocates suggest that you can lead someone to do things through gamification that they would not otherwise be motivated to do. It's a bit like behavior management. While these corporate programs have received positive reviews, they don't seem to have made much impact in public health, personal financial security, or environmentally conservation yet. Does gamification provide the long-term motivation needed to change the behavior of people, including students?

If game mechanics are simply tacked onto an existing learning activity, we may wind up with shallow, novelty effects that are short-lived. But with the ideas below, you may turn the experience of your learning activity into the feel of a real game!

What Is Successful Gamification, and Why Does It Matter?

The dynamics of game-related intrinsic and extrinsic rewards were deeply studied around the 1970's and 80's by Rochester Institute of Technology researchers E.L. Deci and R.M. Ryan (Deci, 1971; Deci & Ryan, 1985). They conducted one kind of study in many variations. They selected a school-related activity that we expect students to enjoy like reading an interesting story. They told one experimental group they were to read a story, and they would be given a reward like money or a gold star when they completed it. They told the other experimental group that they were just to read the interesting story—no reward was mentioned. The real test came when the experimenter was called away by a bogus phone call. He told the students they could continue reading if they want, or they could play one of the interesting games or puzzles on a side table. More of the first group (extrinsic-rewards students) stopped reading and explored the puzzles. More of the second group (no-extrinsic-rewards students) ignored the interesting games and puzzles and continued reading. Did the reward undermine students desire to read?

IMPORTANT: Deci and Ryan's repeated studies found that students tended to lose interest in a task they would otherwise have enjoyed when they receive extrinsic rewards for doing it. Extending this idea to school and reading, we face an uncomfortable possible explanation for the low interest students have in reading after leaving school. The stickers, grades, positive comments and other extrinsic rewards they received in reading instruction during their school careers could undermine the intrinsic fun, joy, and interest in reading they may have otherwise had. Deci and Ryan suggest that the brain confounds the external reward with the intrinsic reward of reading—when the extrinsic reward ends, the brain loses motivation for the task. If you want to learn more about this surprising process, read Daniel Pink's popular book *Drive* (2009) for down-to-earth examples and current research results. Pink suggests that gamification and other extrinsic rewards are needed and good to help adults and children do boring or uninteresting tasks like assembly-line work or math facts practice. Unhappy with their depressing findings, Deci and Ryan continued their studies to see if there are ways to have our extrinsic cake and intrinsically benefit from it too.

In follow-up experiments, Deci and Ryan modified the original studies so that rewards were given immediately to recognize specific positive behaviors, improvements, and milestones (1985). In the new studies, the participants regarded the extrinsic rewards more as *feedback* to inform them of how well they're doing (and when they're unsuccessful). When they received rewards like money for completing a task or receiving a grade, they saw the rewards as a reflection on themselves. When they regarded the rewards as immediate feedback, their brains interpreted the feedback exactly as a game player would interpret when they collect a power-up, add an item to inventory, unlock a puzzle, or complete a level. It's a subtle but critical difference that Chris Aviles captures as he explains how he now focuses on maximizing the learner experience in his classroom just as a game designer does for a positive player experience:

> Before gamification, I designed my classroom around objectives, standards, learning outcomes, and worst of all, assessments. Not once did I consider the student experience in my classroom; not once did I think about what it was like to be a student in my class. Because of gamification, I start with my kids in mind. Thanks to gamification, my classes are designed around having a fun and exciting learning experience first. I look at all the things I have to do as a teacher through the lens of making it as enjoyable as possible for as many students as possible. (Aviles, 2016)

We need to balance extrinsic and intrinsic rewards when we apply gamification principles to learning tasks in order to avoid the negative effects that Margaret Robertson fears in her "Can't Play, Won't Play" blog post (2010): "Gamification is an inadvertent con. It tricks people into believing that there's a simple way to imbue their thing ... with the psychological, emotional and social power of a great game." Let's look at three specific ways to overcome this threat and design activities where gamification benefits learning.

Designing Gamification to Benefit Learning

Sebastian Deterding (2011) is a game and gamification researcher who thinks deeply about how to motivate learners. He identifies three missing ingredients in many gamification attempts that may make the difference between an authentically motivating learning experience and "Snake Oil 2.0". Let's explore his three missing ingredients: **meaning, mastery,** and **autonomy**.

> **Meaning.** Does the gamified task have value for its own sake? If you take away the badges and points, is it still meaningful for students? Would they still do it for the fun of it, continuing to play after school and at home? Gamification works best when it provides feedback toward a personal goal for the user. Can students bring their own interests and curiosity into the learning activity, customizing it to meet their own personal goals? Neuroscience discoveries suggest that without meaning or interest, the brain's powerful learning systems are simply not engaged.

> **Mastery.** In any good game, players are continually learning rules, tactics, and strategies; the emphasis here is continually learning until the skills and achievements of a level are mastered. In *A Theory of Fun for Game Design* (2005), Ralph Koster claims that "Fun is just another word for learning," and fun in games and sports comes from scaffolded mastery. Continually solving problems and puzzles is as addictive as a drug—this is the magic attraction of *Minecraft*. A good game matches the challenge to the zone of proximal development of the

student's learning, and those challenges get continually more complex, more interesting, and more fun as the player gains mastery.

> **Autonomy.** Put students in control to whatever degree possible. Play and games are voluntary. Can you make participation in your gamified activity voluntary? True games allow failure as an integral part of a powerful learning process. Can students play your game without fear of failure? Or does their point score translate into a grade that has consequences outside the game? Do you use points and badges and levels as informational feedback that *helps players achieve personal goals*? The greatest danger of extrinsic rewards is a curbing of autonomy if the students feel the goal is just a way the teacher or school exercises a different kind of control. If students feel that rewards are necessary for them to do the task, then the rewards have devalued the learning activity. It's all in how the students *experience* the gamified activity.

If we follow Detterding's model, we focus on designing a meaningful experience for students, responding to their interests, their intrinsic motivation. We design experiences so they regard them as something they can freely enjoy rather than something that's attempting to control them.

Aviles best expresses the challenging but rewarding path toward meaningful gamification for dedicated teachers:

> I look at all the things I have to do as a teacher through the lens of making it as enjoyable as possible for as many students as possible. ... You can ... create a great gamified classroom just by focusing on the student experience, the amazing intersection where Game Design, Design Thinking and the User Experience meet education. (Aviles, 2016)

Based on my own research and my experience as a K-12 classroom teacher for 20 years and university instructor for over 30 years, I couldn't agree more.

References

Aviles, C. (2016). *The Gamifiation Guide* (Vol 1). Retrieved from TechedUpTeacher.com

Deci, E. L. (1971). Effects of externally mediated rewards on intrinsic motivation. *Journal of Personality and Social Psychology, 18,* 105-115.

Deci, E.L., & Ryan, R. M. (1985). *Intrinsic Motivation and Self-Determination in Human Behavior.* New York: Plenum Press.

Deterding, S. (2011). Meaningful Play: Getting gamification right. *Google Tech Talks*. Retrieved from youtube.com/watch?v=7ZGCPap7GkY

Garrigan, S. R. (1993). *A Comparison of Intrinsic Motivation Elicited in Children by Computer-simulated Robots (Softbots) versus Physical Robots* (Doctoral dissertation) Lehigh University.

Koster, R. (2005). *A Theory of Fun for Game Design*. Sebastapol, CA: O'Reilly Media.

Malone, T. W. (1980). *What Makes Things Fun to Learn? A study of intrinsically motivating computer games*. (Doctoral dissertation) Stanford University.

Malone, T. W., & Lepper, M. R. (1987). Making Learning Fun: A Taxonomy of Intrinsic Motivations for Learning. In R. E. Snow & M. J. Farr (Eds.), *Aptitude, Learning and Instruction III: Conative and Affective Process Analyses* (pp. 223-253).

Pink, D. H. (2009). *Drive: The surprising truth about what motivates us*. New York, NY: Riverhead Books.

Robertson, M. (October, 2010). Can't Play, Won't Play. *Hide & Seek: Inventing new kinds of play*. Downloaded Sept 17, 2016 from hideandseek.net/2010/10/06/cant-play-wont-play/

Schell, J. (2008). *The Art of Game Design: A book of lenses*. Burlington, MA: Morgan Kauffman.

Further Reading

Kapp, K. M. (2012). *The Gamification of Learning and Instruction: Game-based methods and strategies for training and education*. San Francisco, CA: Wiley.

Kapp, K. M., Blair, L., Mesch, R. (2014). *The Gamification of Learning and Instruction Fieldbook: Ideas into practice*. San Francisco, CA: Wiley.

Lorenzo, G. (October, 2016). "University of Michigan turns courses into games." Edsurge News. Retrieved from www.edsurge.com/news/2016-10-20-university-of-michigan-turns-courses-into-games

Rees, D. (August, 2011). "A taxonomy of motivation and game design." Instructional Design Fusion. Retrieved from instructionaldesignfusions.wordpress.com/2011/08/20/a-taxonomy-of-motivation-and-game-design/

Index